# Transforming Prayer

# Transforming Prayer

Praying
to become
rather than
to receive

## Richard O'Ffill

REVIEW AND HERALD® PUBLISHING ASSOCIATION
HAGERSTOWN, MD 21740

This book was
Edited by Lincoln Steed
Copyedited by Jocelyn Fay and James Cavil
Designed by Willie S. Duke
Cover designed by Willie S. Duke
Electronic makeup by Shirley M. Bolivar
Typeset: 11/15 Garamond

PRINTED IN U.S.A.

08  07  06  05  04          7  6  5  4

**R&H Cataloging Service**
O'Ffill, Richard Wesley, 1940-
    Transforming prayer.

    1. Prayer. I. Title

           242

ISBN 0-8280-1397-7

This book is dedicated to my father,
Daniel Wesley O'Ffill,
whose commitment to the Lord
continues to be an inspiration,
and to my dear wife, Betty,
whose encouragement means so much to me.

# Contents

# Introduction

Human beings seem to have a natural tendency to pray. Since the Lord has promised to supply all our needs, we tend to see prayer as something we do when we need something. While people pray about anything and everything, I have observed that when an invitation is made for special prayer requests, most of the petitions tend to center on either physical or financial needs.

There is nothing wrong with praying that the Lord will heal us. The problem is that after we get well, we may neglect to pray.

In the same manner, there is nothing wrong with praying about financial needs. The problem is that if we don't happen to have any needs, we may not pray very much.

Prayer is much more serious to God. Where we might consider prayer an option, something we do when we lose control of a particular aspect of our lives, to God prayer is a condition for carrying out His providence in our lives.

This book is based on the words of our Lord when He admonished us to "seek first the kingdom of God and His righteousness," and also the beautiful word picture from the Spirit of Prophecy that prayer is the "breath of the soul."

The theme and the underlying premise on which this book is based is that the first purpose of prayer is not to *get* but rather to *be*. It is my hope that when you have finished reading, you will see the importance of putting first things first in your prayers. I pray that we all will seek first the kingdom of heaven and His righteousness. In other words, that we will be not as concerned about getting as about being all that the Lord means for us to be. "But what about my physical and material needs?" Don't worry; our Lord has promised that if we will be more concerned about being than about getting, all the other things we have tended to worry about for so long will be added unto us!

Holy Father,

We have been praying for physical and material blessings. Now we are going to go deeper and further than we have been before in our prayers. As we read the thoughts in this book, we are going to pray that You will change us. We are going to pray to be what You have called us to be, Your sons and daughters. We know You will do this for us through the Holy Spirit of our crucified and risen Lord, in whose name we pray.

Amen.

Richard W. O'Ffill, Sr.

# Chapter 1

# Breaking the Routine of Prayer

Have you ever fallen asleep praying by your bedside at night, barely waking up to say "Amen"? I am not asking this to embarrass you or to make you feel guilty. The majority of us have probably fallen asleep in God's presence at some time or another. And it's a common enough failing for our minds to wander so much as we pray that we actually forget what we were praying about!

We say we should make prayer a habit. However, for many of us prayer has become so much a habit that it can become difficult to recognize when we begin or when we end and what we say in between.

A friend once told me that prayer had lost meaning for him. It had become mostly repetition. "Sometimes," he said, "I just close my eyes and say, 'Dear Lord, the same as yesterday!'"

There was the time I was alone at the kitchen table, having lunch. I believe the menu was soup and sandwiches. About halfway through the meal it occurred to me I might not have said the blessing. I thought to myself, *Yes, I think I did*. Then I argued, *But I don't remember what I said, so I probably didn't pray*. Then I reasoned, *I always do pray, but . . .* Well, you can guess what I did. I closed my eyes and prayed again just in case! Sometimes we say we don't think God hears our prayers, but I am afraid, friend, that in many instances we are not listening to our own prayers.

Prayer should be a habit in our lives, but like all habits it can very easily lose significance and become just a routine that we do without thinking. Do you remember putting on your socks this morning? The things we do again and again we soon do without thinking. Prayer can easily become just another thoughtless routine. It should be automatic, but not unconscious.

I must tell you an incident that occurred when I was 5 years old. My mother recently confirmed my recollection of the event; telling me she remembered the day and even the table we were sitting around.

My sister Danna was 2 years old and just beginning to talk. She and I had been playing all morning with a little neighborhood friend. Mother had made arrangements for the little friend to have lunch with us, so we three children sat down around the table.

Mother asked little Danna to say the blessing. We closed our eyes and Danna said, "Deeda pooda pan."

When she said, "Amen," the neighborhood child asked, "What did she say?"

I knew what she had said. I had heard that same prayer many times. I knew she had said, "Dear Jesus, bless this food, amen." But because she said it so often and so fast, it sounded like "Deeda pooda pan!"

Sometimes when I tell this story in my sermons, someone will confess to me afterward, "Pastor O'Ffill, that is where I am in my prayer life. I think I am just saying 'Deeda pooda pan.'" We all face the challenge of making prayer a habit without its becoming a thoughtless routine.

During our first term of mission service in Pakistan, I was asked to go to the Kellogg-Mookerjee Memorial Seminary in Bangladesh to teach a summer session for pastors and teachers. Although Bangladesh is predominantly Muslim, the area around the school has a large Hindu population. I was somewhat familiar with the worship customs of the Muslims, but the Hindu rituals seemed strange and exotic. I remember hearing in the night drums beating hypnotically and the high-pitched chanting of the women. Offerings of one type or another could be seen around what must have been to them holy trees, and of course there were the numerous temples to Hindu gods.

Classes began early in the morning, with a break from noon until 3:00. The weather was hot and sultry, and I found a brief nap during the break could make all the difference.

One afternoon, during my usual "siesta," a thunderstorm rolled through. I didn't mind the sound of the thunder and rain. It actually made my nap more cozy. Waking up and looking out the window, I saw what was left of the dark clouds billowing up in the western sky, heard the sound of distant thunder, and saw lightning flashing dramatically from cloud to cloud. Then, looking at my watch, I noticed it was time to get ready to go back to class.

Then there was a knock at the door of my room. I opened it, and standing there were several of my students. They informed me there was a woman at the gate of the school compound crying and pleading for help. She declared the devil was about to kill one of her children.

From the pastors I found out that the family was Christian—in fact, they were Seventh-day Adventists. Some time previously one of their daughters, who was 13 or 14 years of age, had fallen sick. After the parents tried everything they could think of to make her well, someone suggested they take her to a Hindu priest. Of course, that was not an acceptable option for a Christian family, but because by this time they were desperate, they decided to give it a try. The Hindu priest told the parents she would get well if they would pay the equivalent of one pound of sugar for each pound the girl weighed. Agreeing to the plan, they went home. The girl got well right away. However, the parents couldn't fulfill their part of the bargain because they were too poor. They hardly had enough money to buy food to feed the family.

Some weeks later the young girl went across the river to visit one of her uncles. In the morning she went with some of the other girls to fill their clay pitchers at the village well. As they were letting down the long rope with a bucket tied to one end, the girls were laughing and talking together. Suddenly an evil spirit appeared to the young girl. It told her that unless her parents paid the sugar they owed, it would kill her. The girl became hysterical, dropping her water pitcher to the ground. When the spirit left, she ran crying to her uncle's house, gathered her few things, and asked them to take her home.

Since that incident, the financial condition of the family had not changed, and they still couldn't pay the debt to what was obviously the devil. While I was taking my nap, the girl had been walking along the riverbank in front of the school. Suddenly, out of some bushes on the shore of the river, the evil spirit appeared again. It told her that as she had not paid, she must now die. She collapsed on the ground, unconscious.

Her friends carried her home. The distraught mother ran to the school and stood at the gate, pleading for us to help because the devil was now making good on his promise.

Over the years I had heard of stories in which the devil had either possessed someone or done them harm. I never dreamed one day I would be in the mission field and one of those stories would be happening before my eyes!

I recalled that in the mission stories I had heard or read, there was always a happy ending. The demons were cast out and the victim was delivered. With those stories in mind, I invited the students into my room so we could decide what to do. It can be foolhardy to seek an encounter with the devil, but this situation had come to us, and we couldn't turn the poor woman away.

I knew we had to pray. Some might call it exorcism. But we would have to pray in the name of Jesus and command the devil to come out and leave the girl alone.

Inasmuch as the mission stories I had heard all my life seemed always to tell of successfully casting out devils, I decided I would put together a composite of all the stories. Men will understand better when I say I decided to solve the problem using a "checklist" approach. If you are a woman, think of this as following a type of prayer "recipe."

The first item I looked for was my Bible. I had heard that the devil is afraid of the Bible. So I figured if we carried it along, it would help to scare him away. I found my Bible and mentally checked that item off my list.

The next thing I remembered from the mission stories is that before you go to cast out a devil, you had better pray and confess any sins that might be outstanding on your record. I had heard that if you didn't, the devil might actually name your sins out loud, right there in front of everyone! Something like that actually happened to a friend of mine in New Jersey. One Sabbath a woman possessed by the devil ran down to the front of the church right across the backs of the pews. She jumped down off the front pew and, landing in front of the pastor, began to name his sins to his face.

I couldn't think of anything more that we needed to do right then. I knew that the moment of truth would be the exorcism prayer. I had heard that the devil cannot stand to hear the name of Jesus. If you pronounce the words, "In the name of Jesus, we command the evil spirits to depart," he will go away. At least I was counting on that to happen.

After our prayer of confession, we left for the house nearby where the little girl lived. As we approached, I could hear loud crying. It reminded me of the time Jesus came to the home of the little girl who had just died, and the mourners were making a great deal of noise, as was their custom.

At the house one of our group asked that it be quiet, and soon the loud sound of wailing ceased. Then I saw the girl. She was lying unconscious on the ground by the front door. She was dressed in a green sari, and her hands were folded across her chest. A member of the family asked if we wanted to hear her talk. We asked how that could be. They told us that if they put some kind of leaf under her nose, she would talk. I said I wasn't interested. I imagined that probably we would be hearing the voice of an evil spirit.

Because I was following the "checklist," I realized there was one more thing that needed to be done. The parents had made a huge mistake in entering into a pact with the devil, so I gathered them together and explained the wrong that they had done and asked them to confess it to God. This they did without hesitation.

At last the moment of truth had come. I was sure we had done all the preliminary work that was necessary. All that was left now was the exorcism prayer. We knelt in a half circle around the unconscious girl. The pastor to my left prayed first, in Bengali. When he came to the place where I guessed he was saying, "In the name of Jesus we command these evil spirits to depart," I opened my eyes to see what would happen next. In all the mission stories I could remember, this was the moment the girl would be set free. But nothing happened!

As the next person began to pray, I wondered what detail we had left out. *Surely,* I thought, *we have covered all the bases.* When the second pastor finished praying, I opened my eyes expectantly, but again there was no change.

Then it was my turn to pray. But I was perplexed. It occurred to me that even though we had probably done all the right things leading up to the prayer, the problem was that we were not praying correctly. We must not be saying the right words. So I decided I would try to offer the best prayer I had ever prayed. I would make it long, use lots of big words, and try to say everything in just the right order.

So I closed my eyes and did just that. I don't remember exactly what I said. I do remember I tried to make it a "heavy duty" prayer. I made an effort to use all the right theological words. Finally when I had said all I could think of, the moment of truth had come. So I prayed, "Now in the name of Jesus we command these evil spirits to depart!" I spoke the words loudly and with authority. Surely this would be the thing that had been lacking. Again I opened my eyes, but nothing happened. She was still unconscious.

I will never forget what happened next. Tears began to course down my cheeks uncontrollably. I forgot all the big words, the checklist, and the magic formula. Through my tears I blurted out, "O God, please help us!" The girl opened her eyes as though she had been asleep. I reached down, and taking her by the hand I lifted her up.

Then I understood. You see, I had, as it were, been praying "by the numbers." I was following a checklist. I was treating prayer like some kind of recipe. Though I had followed the right steps and used the right words, I had failed to take into account James 5:16, which says, "The effectual *fervent* prayer of a righteous man availeth much."

Someone once commented that they could see no wrong in falling asleep at night with a prayer on the lips. Of course, there is nothing wrong with that. But it is one thing to fall asleep with a prayer on the lips and another thing to try to pray when we are asleep! My point in this chapter has been to illustrate that for many, prayer has become such a routine that it is little more than a thoughtless reflex action. As we go through this book together, you will discover that we need to get more involved in our prayers. The point is not that we pray more or pray less, but that we learn to pray better!

After each chapter in this book there is a "Reality Check." The purpose of this exercise is to challenge you to evaluate your own prayer experience in the context of what you have just read. Then there will be "hearts-on" prayer exercises—applications of the principles you have just learned. This is called "Fine-tuning Your Prayer Life."

You will not get a letter grade for doing these exercises, but if you will be honest with yourself and with God, you will get a tremendous blessing. We will be going beyond the praying to *get*. Our goal is praying to *be!*

### Doing a Reality Check

1. Do you find yourself repeating certain words or expressions when you pray? If the answer is yes, why do you think this might be?

2. Do you find yourself too often resorting to "canned" prayers (basically the same prayer used at the same occasion)?

3. After reading of my experience in Bangladesh, can you recognize any occasions in your experience in which you might be asking God to do something using a mechanical format?

### Fine-tuning Your Prayer Life

1. Remember what Jesus said about "vain repetitions." When we talk with our friends, we don't usually repeat ourselves or say the same words over and over. Try to pray without using certain words again

and again. (One such word these days in prayers is "just.") This will help us to be aware of what we are saying, and we will be less inclined to resort to a "canned" prayer.

2. The next time you ask the Lord to do something for you, tell Him why you are making that particular request and why it is important to you. Be honest! Doing this helps us to get more involved in our prayers.

### Prayer

Dear Father, thank You for hearing our prayers. Please forgive us when we get so preoccupied with other things that we don't even listen to what we are telling You. Forgive us when we fall into "Deeda pooda pan" prayers.

Teach us to pray without using formulas and practiced prayers. Help us to pray from our hearts, so our prayers to You may always be effective and fervent.

In Jesus' name, amen.

# Chapter 2

# The Secret to Answered Prayer

There are many books telling wonderful answers to prayer. However, books about *unanswered* prayers would fill entire libraries! I am not saying this sarcastically or to tear down our faith in prayer. But for the average person, prayer often seems a waste of time because nothing seems to happen. Faced with a problem, the average Christian will surely pray, but at the same time have "Plan B" ready just in case nothing happens. It is no wonder that for many people prayer has become "The same as yesterday" or "Deeda pooda pan." It seems God never answers their prayers; at least if He does, He always seems to say "No."

Some people take a more optimistic view. They say God answers all their prayers. However, when you ask them what He seems to be saying, they will tell you He says "No" or "Wait" or "Get in line" or "Wrong number." Somehow this lack of cause and effect does not seem to discourage them.

Jesus said more about how to pray than about how to preach. If you review all Jesus had to say about praying, you cannot help getting the distinct impression that whatever you ask in prayer you will receive. Unfortunately, experience tells us it just isn't working that way. We could probably safely say that if God does indeed always answer prayer, then nine times out of ten He seems to say "No."

Some people have no trouble with that. I do. I can't imagine

Jesus encouraging us to pray just so He can say "No." Somehow it just doesn't seem to make sense to me.

Other people say they have figured out the problem. They say if a person prays and nothing happens, it is because they didn't have enough faith. They see faith as a freestanding thing, and if you manage to muster up enough of whatever it is, God will have to do whatever you ask. Personally, I am not comfortable with that explanation of the problem either. I am just as uncomfortable with it as with all the "No" answers. So what to do?

You may find this difficult to believe, but when I ask my wife, Betty, for a favor, nine times out of ten she says "Yes." So whereas on one hand my wife was saying "Yes" to my requests, on the other hand it seemed as though God was mostly saying "No."

I knew it was not a question of who loves whom more. I know Betty loves me very much, but I am sure she doesn't love me more than God does. This being the case, it occurred to me that maybe I could learn something about answered prayer by applying some of the things from my relationship with Betty to my relationship with God.

Betty and I have been married since 1960. When you have lived with a person that long, you get to know them pretty well. As I analyzed what was going on, it dawned on me that before I ask Betty for a favor, I have a pretty good idea of how she is going to respond. If I consider asking her something I have learned she doesn't like, guess what the answer is likely to be? I don't ask!

You may feel that that is cheating. No, it isn't. That is just being smart. Imagine what our marriage would be like if nine times out of ten when I asked her for a favor, or for that matter if she asked me for a favor, the answer were "No." I don't need to tell you what our marriage would be like by now. Is it any wonder that prayer for many people is often a dead-end street, and as a result their relationship with God has suffered?

What is the secret to answered prayer? It is the same as the secret to having your spouse usually say "Yes" when you ask them for a favor. We need to *know God*. For this reason we must learn to pray as Jesus meant for us to pray or we will not be able to "grow in grace, and in the *knowledge* of our Lord and Saviour, Jesus Christ" (2 Peter 3:18).

Now, here is where things can seem for a moment to get complicated. A person may say, "But it is easy to know your spouse. You live with them, you can see them and touch them and talk with them. But how can a person get to know God? He is invisible."

Don't give up or be discouraged. Let's follow it through. We are on the track of something. Jesus has not left us on our own in this regard.

The answer to all of these questions is found in Matthew 6. Take a few minutes sometime and read the whole chapter. Just in case you don't have your Bible next to you, allow me to help you consider a few verses from Matthew 6:26-33: "Behold the fowls of the air: for they sow not, neither do they reap, nor gather into barns; yet your heavenly Father feedeth them. Are ye not much better than they?

"Which of you by taking thought can add one cubit unto his stature?

"And why take ye thought for raiment? Consider the lilies of the field, how they grow; they toil not, neither do they spin:

"And yet I say unto you, That even Solomon in all his glory was not arrayed like one of these.

"Wherefore, if God so clothe the grass of the field, which today is, and tomorrow is cast into the oven, shall he not much more clothe you, O ye of little faith?

"Therefore take no thought, saying, What shall we eat? or, What shall we drink? or, Wherewithal shall we be clothed?

"(For after all these things do the Gentiles seek:) for your heavenly Father knoweth that ye have need of all these things.

"But seek ye first the kingdom of God, and his righteousness; and all these things shall be added unto you."

Friend, in these verses Jesus is setting priorities for our prayers!

Notice what He says. "Therefore take no thought, saying, What shall we eat? or, What shall we drink? or, Wherewithal shall we be clothed?"

I am going to ask you a personal question. Think for a moment of what you usually pray about. If you are like most of us, you are probably praying about what Jesus said we ought *not* worry about. The focus of our prayers tends to be on what I call "the flesh and its support groups." Jesus says we should not be worrying about the material things of our lives, but in reality this is exactly what most of us are hung up on. Nine times out of ten it is the material aspects of our lives that we pray about most. Can you see it now? It is not that He doesn't care about whether we have food and clothes and a place to live. You notice He says, "Your heavenly Father knoweth that ye have need of all these things."

As a rule, what Jesus says ought to be our priority in prayer usually isn't. Jesus asks us to seek first the kingdom of heaven and His righteousness. This, He tells us, should be what we pray for above all else. Of course, for some people, the kingdom of heaven and His righteousness can sound mystical. It doesn't sound like a "hands-on" kind of prayer.

But Jesus does not leave us stranded or confused. He explains what the kingdom of heaven is and what it isn't. Notice this next text. First it tells us what the kingdom of heaven isn't, and then it tells us what it is. "The kingdom of God is not in *meat* and *drink;* but *righteousness,* and *peace,* and *joy* in the Holy Ghost" (Rom. 14:17).

This text tells us that the kingdom of heaven is not about material things. The text tells us the kingdom of heaven is about righteousness, peace, and joy in the Holy Ghost.

If you want to reveal your habit of praying for what Jesus tells us not to worry about, try to remember what your 10 most recent prayers have been about. If you are like most people, you will see immediately that the burden of our prayers tends to be exactly what we are counseled not to worry about. Isn't this incredible?

Notice this thought in the book *Gospel Workers,* pages 254 and 255: "Prayer is the breath of the soul. It is the secret of spiritual power. No other means of grace can be substituted, and the health of the soul be preserved. Prayer brings the heart into immediate contact with the Wellspring of life, and strengthens the sinew and muscle of the religious experience.

"Neglect the exercise of prayer, or engage in prayer spasmodically, now and then, as seems convenient, and you lose your hold on

22

God. The spiritual faculties lose their vitality, the religious experience lacks health and vigor."

Comparing prayer to the process of breathing makes it very clear. We don't breathe to *get,* we breathe to *be!* Likewise, the priority of prayer is to pray to be, not to get. Jesus tells us to seek first the kingdom of heaven and His righteousness, which is love, joy, and peace. In other words, it is about who we are, not what we can get. Prayer is the breath of the soul, in that it is the process by which we constantly seek to be the kind of men and women God means for us to be.

Some people have told me that they don't pray just for things; they tell me they pray for their children and their family. Of course, it is important and necessary that we pray for our children and family. But a danger may be that we are praying that God will change everyone else's life but our own. A person may be praying, "O Lord, please change my wife; if You do, I won't be so mean to her." We don't really say it, but the implication is that I am treating someone else a certain way because of the way they are treating me; and if the Lord will just change them, I will be able to treat them as I ought. In the same way, a mother might pray, "Lord, my children drive me crazy; help them to be good children so I won't scream at them so much."

Someone has rightly said life is 10 percent what happens to us and 90 percent how we react to it. Yet it seems most of us tend to focus our prayers on the 10 percent, asking God to change what is happening to us, rather than on the 90 percent.

You might be thinking by now, *But you don't know my spouse or my children. I need to trade them in and get new ones!* Do you really want to have a new family? Try praying that God will change *you,* and you will get a new spouse and new children. We must not forget that other people are reacting to the way we are, just as we are reacting to the way they are.

One day someone asked me if praying for oneself is not selfish praying. I answered that it depended on what we were praying for. If we are praying to get rich and powerful or become beautiful or handsome, that would be selfish praying. But if we are praying the Lord will forgive us for our selfishness, pride, bitterness, lust, and lack of self-control, and in their place give us the fruit of the Spirit, which is love, joy, peace, long-suffering, gentleness, goodness, faith, meekness, and self-control, that is not selfish praying at all, but prioritizing our prayers as Jesus asked us to do. It is what He meant when He told us to seek first the kingdom of heaven and His righteousness.

Since coming to understand prayer as something I do to be and not to get, my perspective on life has changed drastically. You see, a person who is praying to get rich may feel God doesn't love them if they should for some reason fall on hard times. In the same way, a person who is praying for a promotion on the job may feel rejected by both God and other people if they are passed over for the promotion.

In contrast, a person seeking first the kingdom of heaven and His righteousness is the person who can understand perfectly the meaning of Romans 8:28: "And we know that *all things work together for good* to them that love God, to them who are the called according to his purpose." The person who is praying to *be* rather than to *get* cannot grow in the things that have to do with the development of character.

A person who has not learned to seek first the kingdom of heaven and His righteousness can even find themselves praying prayers that cancel each other out. We often pray that the Lord will bless us. By that we mean that we will be spared problems and have just the things we need. Later we may find ourselves praying that the Lord will give us patience. This is like praying out of two sides of our mouth. Let me explain. Who is more likely to be an impatient person, the one accustomed to getting their way or the person who has learned to live with frustrations? It is obvious: a patient person is one who has learned to live with problems and frustrations. If we pray that everything will go our way and in the next breath pray that the Lord will give us patience, these prayers in effect cancel each other out! How could the Lord give us patience without permitting us to endure frustrations and delays?

Have you ever prayed that the Lord would make you humble? You had better be ready for trouble if you pray that prayer and really mean it. The curriculum for humility is to suffer humiliation.

I am convinced that the spiritual graces of love, compassion, forgiveness, and all the rest can be developed only through suffering. Though it is obvious that while we do not generally ask for suffering, we must not occupy our prayers in seeking to avoid suffering and trials. To do so is to make it impossible for the Lord to develop in us the qualities of love, joy, and peace—characteristics of the kingdom of heaven.

Understanding this principle, we can appreciate the promise that "there is no temptation [trial] taken us but such as is common to man, but He will with the temptation [trial] make a way of escape, that we might be able to bear it" (1 Cor. 10:13, paraphrased). To "make a way to escape" does not necessarily mean to make it disappear, but rather, as the text says, to enable us to bear it.

So the secret of having more "Yes" answers than "No" answers to our prayers is to seek first the kingdom of heaven. In doing this we learn to know God and understand that in all things He is working for our good (Rom. 8:28).

Before you proceed to the reality check and the fine-tuning, you might want to reread the chapter. This chapter and the one following are foundational to the premise of this book. We know how to pray to get. Now we are going to go beyond and learn *what it means to pray to be.*

### Doing a Reality Check

1. Take a moment to analyze your prayers. Is there a reoccurring theme? What are you usually praying about?

2. Have you noticed you pray a lot more about sickness and/or financial problems than you do about the kind of person you are?

3. When you ask that God will work in the life of a loved one, do you include yourself in the prayer? In what way?

4. Do you pray as much when there are fewer things to worry about as when there are a lot of problems? If the answer is "No," what might this signify?

### Fine-tuning Your Prayer Life

1. The next time you pray for a wayward loved one, think

about some things God might need to do in your life to make it possible to answer your prayer. Ask the Lord to change your life in those specific areas.

2. The next time you have physical or other material problems in your life, think of how these experiences might help you to *be* a better person. Try thanking God for them. Thank Him specifically for what these painful and difficult experiences have taught you.

### Prayer

Holy Father, You know we need food and clothing and a place to live. You have told us not to worry about those things so much because You have promised that as You provide for the birds, You know our physical needs and will provide for us as well.

Forgive us for being more worried about our houses and jobs and clothes and all the rest than we are about the kind of people we are.

Lord, from this moment on may every experience in our lives, both the good and the bad, the happy and the sad, draw us closer and closer to You. You promised that all things will work together for good to them that love You. We love You, Jesus. Amen.

# Chapter 3

# Understanding the Purpose of Prayer

P rayer is important! The Son of God Himself became our prayer teacher. I love reading Luke 11, which begins, "And it came to pass, that, as he was praying in a certain place, when he ceased, one of his disciples said unto him, Lord, teach us to pray, as John also taught his disciples."

Jesus then gave what is called the Lord's Prayer. Most of us learn this prayer when we are very young. It is usually a prayer we pray in unison. I don't know why we developed this custom, because it is a wonderful prayer to pray when one is alone. Of course, it can easily become a ritual prayer, part of a prayer habit. If we are not careful, it can lose meaning.

After much study and analysis of this prayer, I am thrilled to realize Jesus taught it not just as something to repeat, but as a "template" for us to construct our individual prayers. That is why it is called the Model Prayer.

In this chapter we are going to look at the first part of the prayer. Looking at the concepts and principles behind its wonderful words will help us to understand the purpose of prayer.

### *"Our Father Which Art in Heaven"*

These words tell us whom we are praying to and what *relationship* we have to Him. It is sad that in this day and age the word "Father" can conjure up all kinds of negative emotions for some people. This is because the devil has been so successful in breaking up and nearly obliterating much that is precious and sacred about human existence. Within the family relationships God meant for us to understand in part our relationship to Him. Ruin the home and it can severely distort a person's concept of God. When the family is in disarray, it can cause huge barriers to fall across our hearts and keep us from knowing and understanding God as our heavenly Father.

In spite of the sorrows that many have suffered in the earthly family, Jesus teaches us that when we pray, we are talking to the father every child in their heart of hearts wishes they had and which we do, in fact, have in Him. Our heavenly Father understands things about us we don't even understand about ourselves. He knows what is best for us and will, if we will allow Him, cause all things to work together for good in our lives. That doesn't mean everything that happens to us will feel good, but in spite of what happens to us, He will eventually bring something good out of it.

When we pray, our heavenly Father assures us that He hears us. More and more large companies are automating their phone answering systems. It is getting to the place where you can call a company, carry on a conversation, give information, and get information in return, all without human contact. A voice will say "Thank you" and "Have a good day." The caller has actually been conversing with a computer chip!

When Jesus taught us to pray, He wanted to set the record straight. He wanted us to know from the very first that when we pray, we are not talking to a computer chip or somebody who will try to take advantage of us, but to a Being to whom we can relate as a kind and loving father and who relates to us as His children.

### *"Hallowed Be Thy Name"*

Our heavenly Father is something that no father on this earth has ever been, and that is completely holy. When we say "Hallowed be Thy name," we are not giving Him a wonderful compliment; rather, we are acknowledging what He is.

We need to study more and more the meaning of holiness. We

often contemplate the love of God, His mercy, His grace, His faithfulness, and His goodness, but we will not be able to truly appreciate these wonderful revelations of our heavenly Father until we catch a glimpse of His holiness.

Without becoming theological or philosophical, we can grasp the importance of His holiness by seeing that His mercy and grace, His faithfulness and goodness, are *how* He is, while holy is *what* He is. Inasmuch as He is first and foremost holy, we must discover what holy means, or we could end up praying to a god who doesn't exist or find ourselves worshiping a god of our own imagination.

All the idols that have ever been made are the results of missing the point of the true holy nature of God. When we don't know the truly holy God, we do the next best thing, and that is we make gods who are just like us.

Our heavenly Father is holy, so when we pray, "Our Father which art in heaven, hallowed be Thy name," we don't need to have flashbacks of some sad or disappointing relationship we may have had with our father here on earth. Rather, when we say, "Hallowed be Thy name," we can know we are talking to our heavenly Dad, whose holiness results in His doing everything just as it should be done.

I say our heavenly Dad because that is what Jesus called Him while He was in the Garden of Gethsemene. "And He said, 'Abba, Father, all things are possible unto thee; take away this cup from me: nevertheless not what I will, but what thou wilt'" (Mark 14:36). The word "Abba" means the equivalent of "daddy." Jesus called our heavenly Father "Daddy," and we can do the same. I called a Jewish rabbi and asked him about the word Abba. He told me that is what little children in Israel call their fathers even today!

This concept gives special meaning then to Romans 8:15: "For ye have not received the spirit of bondage again to fear; but ye have received the Spirit of adoption, whereby we cry, Abba [Daddy], Father." Similarly Galatians 4:6: "Because ye are [sons and daughters] God hath sent forth the Spirit of his Son into your hearts, crying, Abba, Father."

### "Thy Kingdom Come"

Having taught us to pray to God as our Holy Father, Jesus now teaches that we are to pray, "Thy kingdom come." I have never lived in a country where there was a ruling king. Once, though, I traveled through Iran when that country did have a king (the shah). His Royal Highness' picture was on every wall and his statue in every square. With a very few exceptions kings and queens in modern times have virtually no personal authority over the people.

With God this is not the case. For those who live in countries where there is a democratic form of government this idea may be difficult to comprehend, and some may even be uncomfortable with it, yet we must understand that the government of God is not a democracy. In countries where there are monarchies today, the citizens often have the constitutional right to abolish the royal family if they so choose. But in the kingdom of God this could never happen. While in this age a king gets his power from the people, it is just the opposite in the kingdom of heaven. God's people get their very being and existence from the heavenly King.

When we say "Thy kingdom come," we are acknowledging that God is our king. This concept goes further than His being our heavenly Father. It not only means He's our Father, but that we acknowledge Him as our ruler. We accept His word as law.

Here is where many often have a problem in their relationship to God. They don't mind seeing God as daddy, especially if daddy is a figure who gives you everything you want and you have him wrapped around your little finger. But they may well resist the reality that God is the one who tells them how to live.

If we truly are going to understand the purpose of prayer, we need to have a clear concept of God not only as our holy Father but also as our king, our ruler. He is not our president, our representative, our coordinator, or our facilitator. He is our God, and when we say "Thy kingdom come," we are saying we willingly acknowledge Him as king in our lives.

### "Thy Will Be Done"

Understanding that God, who relates to us as a father, is holy, we acknowledge Him as more than a father; He is our maker and our God. We are now able to go on to understand that *the purpose of prayer is to discover the will of God and to receive the grace to obey it.* When we say "Thy will be done," we are declaring that as far as our lives are concerned, we will do it His way.

An evangelist friend of mine told me that sometimes he will ask the people, "How many of you are tired of someone telling you what to do?" He declares most people will raise their hands in the affirmative. Then he will say with a smile, "Well, I guess I am wasting my time preaching the gospel to you!"

You see, a person who has a hard time relating to authority will have a hard time relating to God. Sin is about having our own way. It is about not letting God tell us what to do. The whole purpose of the plan of salvation is to bring us back to the point where we will willingly and gladly be able to say again, "I delight to do Your will, O my God; yes, You have written Your law in my heart" (Ps. 40:8, paraphrased). When we say "Thy will be done," we are actually committing ourselves to do His will.

It may be disappointing to some to learn that our prayers must not be to get God to do what we want Him to do, but rather to discover what He wants us to do. So often when we pray we come to God with our minds already made up. We not only tell Him what is wrong; we tell Him what to do about it and when to be finished. Scripture tells us we don't know how to pray as we should (Rom. 8:26). Is it any wonder that Jesus' disciples asked Him to teach them to pray?

I have known people who thought when we pray, if we say "Thy will be done," it is a sign of resignation. Kind of like giving up! They think if a person has enough faith, God is obliged to do what they want Him to. Some say we should look through the Bible, find the promise of God that suits our need or desire at the particular time, then "name it and claim it." We ought to be careful about this method. I am not convinced every particular thing God did for somebody at some time or other is necessarily His will for me at this present time.

There are others who may think that if God knows what is best for us and will do only what He wants to do anyway, why bother to pray at all? While He will do only His will, He wants us to be partners in the endeavor. Prayer must be our initiative. After all, God has given us the power of choice.

Some kind of choice, you may say! That is like saying you either do what He wants or you don't do it at all. But wait. When we understand whom we are praying to, we wouldn't want it to be any other way. Our heavenly Father wants far better things for us than we could ever conceive for ourselves. Remember the text that says that "eye has not seen nor ears heard, neither has entered into our hearts even the idea of the wonderful things that God has prepared for those who love him" (1 Cor. 2:9, paraphrased).

After reading this chapter a person might say, "Does this mean then that I have been praying wrong all my life?" Not to worry! God is not sitting up there in heaven trying to tag us out on some technicality; neither does He discount our best efforts. In calling heaven from our heart of hearts, it is possible to get through even when we dial a wrong number! God reads the intents and desires of our hearts and is gracious and merciful. He is always on our frequency. He knows our hearts. The problem is that we are not always on His frequency, and therein lies our challenge in learning to pray.

Isn't Jesus a wonderful prayer teacher? When we enroll in the school of prayer with Him and attend faithfully, two things happen. One is that we never graduate, and the other is that we will never fail! I love the prayer text that is a kind of safety net. "Likewise the Spirit also helpeth our infirmities: for we know not what we should pray for as we ought: but the Spirit itself maketh intercession for us with groanings which cannot be uttered. And he that searcheth the hearts knoweth what is the mind of the Spirit, because he maketh intercession for the saints according to the will of God" (Rom. 8:26, 27). Isn't that a wonderful promise!

### Doing a Reality Check

1. Are you comfortable calling God your heavenly Daddy? If there are problems with this, could it be you need to ask God to help you deal with some bitterness and resentment?

2. Are you asking God to do things inconsistent with His holiness? What would those requests be like?

3. How do you feel about God being the absolute authority in your life? How should this affect your everyday life?

4. Are you willing to say "Thy will be done" and mean it?

### Fine-tuning Your Prayer Life

1. Make sure there is nothing in your relationship with your earthly father that would make it difficult for you to relate to a heavenly Father. If you discover there are some problems, ask God for the wonderful gift of forgiveness.

2. Get a Bible concordance and look up the word "holy." Read the texts that refer to the holiness of God. Make sure you have a clear concept as to what the Bible means when it says that God is holy.

3. Tell God you are willing to do His will in every aspect of your life. Think of specific changes that need to be made to bring this about.

### Prayer

Holy Father in heaven, please forgive me for sometimes trying to get You to do what I want done rather than what You want. I've sometimes asked You to do things that are incompatible with who You are. Sometimes I've even resented having to say "Thy will be done."

We know we could never want something better for ourselves than what You would want for us. In the future when I say "Thy will be done," I will really mean it from my heart.

Your Son/Daughter,

(your name)

# Chapter 4

# Discovering the Will of God

We have learned that the purpose of prayer is to discover and to do the will of God. This concept should reassure us, because our holy God, the Creator of heaven and earth, would never desire for us anything that was not for our long-range good, as well as for His glory.

One of the problems that we must overcome when we pray is the natural tendency to want God to do us a favor, to give us special treatment. We are often aware that what we are asking is sometimes a little bit "special," but we hope that He will make an exception for our case. Although God is always ready to hear sincere prayers, He is not always ready to become involved in some of the things that people ask Him to do for them. Nevertheless, many hope that He is so glad to hear from them that He will give them a special break and maybe give them an answer that is more to their liking than to His. We easily forget that the purpose of prayer is not to get Him to do what we want but to bring our lives into line with what He wants for us.

This tension between His will and ours doesn't change His mind, but it can easily cause a person to become discouraged and begin to believe that prayer is futile. They can even become frustrated with the whole thing and say "God doesn't hear my prayers," when in fact He hears every prayer. Many prayers are so "far out" that He seems not to be paying any attention to us. We need to realize that if God answered our selfish prayers, He would be encouraging our selfishness. If He answered our proud requests in our favor, He would actually be affirming our pride.

We can resolve these tensions and actually save ourselves a lot of frustration and disappointment if we *discover what the will of God is before we pray.*

Suppose that a family decides to design a house. Although they can decide what they want their house to look like, where every room is to be, and what the amenities will include, there is a point at which the customizing must stop. There is a limit as to how far made-to-order house plans can go.

Although the family can decide how many rooms the house will have and how it will look, all of their plans and ideas will in the final analysis be subject to the building codes. Even though it will be their house design, how it is built and the context in which it is built will not depend on them but on the building codes.

It is the same way when we take our plans to God in prayer. We may want Him to "customize" our lives, and indeed He will. But He will do that only within the context of and in conformity to His "codes."

God can say "Yes" to our prayers only when they are in harmony with His codes. By this I mean in harmony with His will. It is important to know that He doesn't make up the rules as He goes along. When someone applies for a building permit, it is sometimes possible to receive a variance or an exception to the code; however, when we pray we should not expect that God will give us a variance or an exception to His code.

You have probably guessed by now that the Bible is God's codebook, and the codes that are found in His Word take precedence over all the "customized plans" we may have for our own lives. To be successful in prayer *we must begin by accepting the Bible as the revealed will of God.* If a person insists on praying that God will do something for them that is not in harmony with the principles of Scripture, they are wasting their time.

The famous nineteenth-century English preacher Charles

Spurgeon was once invited to a major social event that included a big banquet. As it happened, there in the middle of the table of food was a roasted pig. The host of the occasion asked Spurgeon to say the blessing over the food they were about to eat. Eyeing the big porker on the table, the preacher closed his eyes and prayed, "Lord, if You can bless what You have already cursed, please bless this food."

Now, that may not have been the politically correct thing for him to do, but it was surely correct theologically. It is quite possible that unless we are careful we could actually be praying that God will bless something in our lives that He has already cursed!

Just as a person who designs a house and wants to avoid disappointment and added expense will find out what the code permits and what the zoning laws governing the area will allow, so we must realize God has already saved us a lot of time and trouble by giving us His Word. This means that when we go to Him in prayer, we must always pray in harmony with what He has already revealed in His Word. A person who is not into the Word of God will not be able to pray effectively. Their prayers will tend to be hit-and-miss, trial-and-error.

There are people who have studied the Sabbath and become convicted that it is the true day of rest. But then they say that they are praying that God will reveal whether He wants them to keep it or not. Bless their hearts, He has already revealed it to them through His Word. This is not a matter of discovering what the will of God is, but rather of praying for grace to obey it.

I am not comfortable when a person says they are waiting for God to tell them something inside their hearts, a kind of inner voice. This can be very dangerous. There are many people who are under the impression that God doesn't hold them accountable or responsible unless they themselves happen to agree with what is in the Bible. They seem to think an obedient relationship with God is like a contract, and if they haven't signed up, it is not binding.

A person who continues to pray and is knowingly disobedient to something obvious in the Word of God is either already in trouble or is headed for big trouble in their spiritual life. The Scriptures tell us that because people would not believe the truth, God gives them over to an illusion that they might believe a lie and be damned (see 2 Thess. 2:11, 12).

Let's return to the illustration of the family that wants to custom build a house. In addition to building codes there is also the matter of zoning regulations and community covenants. The building codes are the rules that govern the construction of the building itself. The zoning regulations and the covenants are the standards that have to do with the well-being of the community as a whole.

In the community where I live the community association doesn't permit us to park a camping trailer in the driveway. When we first moved into our house, we had a pop-up trailer. I parked it in the driveway temporarily, as the garage was full of packing boxes. One day I received a letter from the community association advising me that I could not do that. The letter explained that the covenants of the community forbade it. Where we live the residents must also keep their grass cut and cannot paint their house an outlandish color. The community association insists that its residents abide by the standards established in the covenants.

One of the fundamental issues we have in our prayer experience that is many times we have not bought into God's standard of righteousness for our lives. By that I mean His standard of right and wrong.

When someone has a standard for themselves that is not God's standard for them, when they bring a problem to Him in prayer, they tend to want only a quick fix. Like the old-timer used to say: "I fixed it with chewing gum and baling wire!" The tendency is to request a superficial answer to prayer. Some are satisfied to have their lives fixed with parts from the junkyard because they are cheaper than the genuine replacement parts.

This may be caused in part because we live in a "take away the pain" society. Our tendency is to treat the symptoms. It's as though we are saying, "Just give me a Tylenol now, Lord, and I'll try to remember to call You in the morning."

We need to understand that when we feel pain and guilt, it means there are fundamental causes that need to be addressed. Of course we need to take our guilt and pain to the Lord, but only with a view of having the Holy Spirit perform an MRI so we can learn the cause of the problem.

The closer we can come to holding ourselves to the standard that God has for us, the more our prayers will be according to His will. God will be satisfied only when we are cleansed from all unrighteousness, and we ourselves must be satisfied with nothing less.

The Bible is clear in revealing what is God's standard for us. That standard is that we be conformed to the image of His Son (Rom. 8:29). This should be the priority in all our prayers.

We should not be upset or feel intimidated by God's high standard for us. No one is upset to say they will not be satisfied until they are a millionaire or until they are the president of a large company. What is wrong with God's wanting us to be free from sin and filled with the fruit of the Spirit? We must not feel that we will never be able to attain this high ideal, because He has promised that inasmuch as He has begun a good work in us, He will finish it (Phil. 1:6)!

If this seems a little bit overwhelming, think of it this way. I learned to speak Spanish. I don't speak it perfectly or without an accent, but I can communicate effectively. So though we don't speak God's language perfectly, we are learning to communicate with Him. As we read His Word we learn more and more of His will to guide us as we pray.

Someone might ask, "Should I stop praying until I have it all figured out?" I hope not. We are His children. We are learning to speak His language, and along the way God listens to our every word. He knows our hearts and our needs. But to pray effectively we must learn to know our hearts too and also learn to know His. We must learn our real needs and how He has promised to supply them.

The Reality Check and the Fine-tuning that follow each chapter are not to put us on some kind of guilt trip. It is sin that has put us on a guilt trip. As we learn more and more about the will of God, and as we pray more and more according to His will, we will experience what the Scripture means when it says, "There is therefore now no condemnation to them which are in Christ Jesus" (Rom. 8:1).

### Doing a Reality Check

1. Are you praying God will bless something in your life He has already cursed?

2. Are any of your current prayers about symptoms or are you aware of the underlying problems? Can you think of any specifics?

### Fine-tuning Your Prayer Life

1. Write down three specific things you have been asking the Lord to do for you. Then discover from the Bible what principle applies to each request. How will this knowledge affect your prayers? (Remember, we tend to see things from a much narrower perspective than God does.)

2. Choose a particular problem you have been praying about. Discover if it is a symptom or a cause. If it is a symptom, discover from the Word of God what the cause might be. (For example, you have been praying God will help you with a financial problem. You may discover covetousness is leading you to excessive buying.)

### Prayer

Heavenly Daddy, You have been very gracious with us not to leave us to find our way alone. Thank You for the Bible. Thank You for the people You chose to write it. Thank You for the Spirit of Prophecy, which helps us to understand what it means at a time when there seems to be so much confusion.

Lord, You are also the King of the universe. We want to pray about what You want us to pray about. We want You to convict us of what we really need so that we can ask You to do it for us. Help us to pray about the things that matter most to You.

We love You, and we know that You love us.

In Jesus' name, amen.

# Chapter 5

# Essential Attitudes

I came home from work one day and discovered that the phone line was completely dead. Testing the box where the line enters our house, I found the incoming line was as dead as the proverbial doornail. Using another phone, I called the company, and they sent out a technician, who confirmed the line to the house was dead. This line runs underground from where it enters the house to a place at the back of our property line. We could not figure out what had happened, because the line was alive at the property line but dead where it entered the house.

Then we discovered that a neighbor had installed a fence the day before and had inadvertently cut the underground line. The phone man put in a temporary line, and the following week he returned to make the repair permanent. The problem was solved.

The success of a company can depend on its service. We tend to do the most business with a company that gives not only the best price but also the best service. I suspect this mentality sometimes carries over into our concept of prayer. We tend to see praying to God as the ultimate service call.

When we call a service representative to fix the washing machine, or when we take our car in to be repaired, it isn't a requirement to be a personal friend of the person who does the repairs. In fact, if a person feels they are not getting the service they deserve, they might even file a complaint with the management. While this attitude might be acceptable in doing business, it can be damaging to our relationship with God, and it will render the prayer life ineffective.

The purpose of prayer, as we have already seen, is not to persuade God to serve us. Prayer is an act of our coming to Him with a desire to do His will. There has never been a problem in God's attitude toward us, though the devil has tried to persuade us otherwise. As our heavenly Father, He cares for us more than we care for ourselves, and He knows what we need even better than we do ourselves.

God created us to glorify Him and for His pleasure (Eph. 2:10). One person I shared this concept with seemed to have a little trouble with this. His question was "But what about my happiness? If I am always trying to make God happy, when will I have the occasion to enjoy myself?" My friend, making God happy and glorifying His name should make us happy ourselves. The significance and meaning of our entire existence—our present and ultimate happiness—is wholly in proportion to the extent to which we do His will and serve Him.

If we tend to see prayer as a type of service call, we will consider it something to be done mechanically or by the numbers. Many seem to think that if we pray this way or say it that way, it will work for us. Or if it is not working, we just need to try using different words. The priority of prayer is not about *doing,* it is about *being.* No matter how technically correct our prayers may be, if our attitude is not right it will be all for nothing.

Sin is about wrong attitudes. Wrong attitudes will always lead to wrong actions. Only right actions will change wrong attitudes. And yes, it is possible to do the right thing for the wrong reason. We may be able to think of a thousand needs we have or a thousand problems that beset us. But our greatest need is to have a new attitude. You may have noticed that life's most serious problems are usually the result of our wrong attitudes. Has someone ever said to you, "I don't like your attitude"? The more I look into the depths of my own heart, the more I realize I don't like my attitudes. When certain things happen, our initial reaction is usually sadness and disappointment. But then bitterness and resentment begin to set in. I could mention anger and frustration. So often these are followed by shame and embarrassment.

Our gut reaction to life's trials can easily be "Why are they doing this to me?" "Where did I fail?" "What will people think of me?" I am finally realizing I have spent a lot of time praying God would change the world and less time praying He would change me and give me a right attitude. I believe I am beginning to get my priorities straight. In the process, I am seeing some incredible miracles.

I can't tell you of someone raised to life from the dead, or of receiving a check in the mail for just the amount needed the day the bank was to foreclose. But I can tell you for certain God is doing wonderful things in changing my heart. He is not finished with me yet, but I can truly testify to the Bible promise that in Him old things pass away and all things become new (2 Cor. 5:17). I'm not talking about a new house, a new car, a new wardrobe, or even a new body. I'm talking about new hearts and new attitudes.

### *The Attitude of Praise*

We must pray God will give us the attitude of praise. True praise is an attitude before it is an act. A person who doesn't have an inward attitude of praise cannot really praise God outwardly. What good would it do? God doesn't look on the outside; He looks on the heart (1 Sam. 16:7).

To give praise to God is to give Him the credit. Someone who doesn't have an attitude of praise may go through all the motions, but what they will be giving is flattery, not praise. Flattery is insincere praise.

We are quick to ask God to do a favor for us. However, many times we are slow to give Him the credit for answering our prayers. How many times do we pray that God will heal a sick friend or loved one, and when they get well there is often nothing more said. Or worse, there may be some comment about how good the hospital was or how skillful the doctors who gave the treatments were!

Many of us pray before we take a trip and ask God to keep us safe. Then, when we arrive safe and sound, we forget all about our prayer.

When Scripture says, "Oh that men would praise the Lord for his goodness" (Ps. 107:8), it is not referring to clapping, shouting, beating drums, dancing, raising hands, or even saying "Amen." A person can easily go through the motions of praising God and yet not have an attitude of praise. True praise must begin in the heart. Rather than praying for God to teach us how to praise Him, we need first to pray He will develop in us the attitude of praise.

There has been an increasing tendency to bring God down to our level. I remember one song entitled "Have You Talked With the Man Upstairs?" In casual conversations I have heard God referred to as the "Big Man." A high school football team somewhere named the Cougars prayed to the Big Cougar in the sky before every game.

Talking with a young man about spiritual things, I was told that he and "JC" got along pretty good. If we can rise no higher than our concept of God, what will be the end of us if our God is the "Man upstairs," the "Big Man," "JC," or the "Big Cougar in the sky"?

We cannot receive a correct attitude of praise if we have a low concept of God. As long as we insist on bringing God down to our level, two things will result. One, we will not be lifted out of our present fallen condition, and two, we will not be able to praise God as He deserves—yes, as He must be praised.

### Jesus Calls Us to Consecration

Another essential attitude is consecration. Jesus prayed, "Consecrate them in truth. For their sakes I consecrate Myself, that they themselves also may be consecrated in the truth" (John 17:17-19, paraphrased).

A person who is not consecrated to God cannot pray effectively. When we pray "Thy will be done," we indicate that we are consecrated and dedicated to do His will no matter what the cost.

Prayer cannot be an arm's-length transaction with God. We do business every day with strangers. We do it within the context of law and convention. It is possible to do business with a person and not even like them if they have what we want badly enough. With God this is an impossible relationship. Prayer is not doing business with God.

Scripture says those who come to God "must believe that he is, and that he is a rewarder of them that diligently seek him" (Heb. 11:6). When we come to Him in prayer, we must sooner or later be totally consecrated to Him. To be consecrated to Him means to be committed to doing His will.

To obey God and to do God's will are the same thing. It is unfortunate that so few understand that doing the will of God is the same as obeying Him. The concept of obedience is seen by many to be legalistic. A person who is not consecrated to God may be obedient in a limited mechanistic way, but will probably not enjoy it. On the other hand, a person who is consecrated wants to obey God in every aspect of their lives and actually enjoys doing it! (Ps. 40:8).

We need to be continually renewing our consecration to the Lord if we are to pray effectively. A person may ask why we need to commit to the Lord continually. Their question puts me in mind of the man who in 30 years hadn't told his wife that he loved her. When a friend asked him why, he answered, "I told her 30 years ago I loved her, and nothing has changed."

Though we may not realize it, things do change. When we drive, we have to keep our hands on the steering wheel continually. It may be the same driver; it may be the same car. It is the road that changes; and if we are not committed to driving, we are sure to run off the road.

Because we live in a world of sin (sin is outside of us and inside of us), we must keep our consecration up-to-date. It is our consecration that reaches out to God when temptation comes along. When I am tempted, I remind myself of my consecration to the Lord, and He gives me the grace to overcome.

Driving down the road not long ago, an "off-the-wall" temptation came into my mind. When I realized I was being tempted, I said to myself, "Oh, I could never do that. My consecration to Christ does not permit that sort of thing." When this thought came to my heart, I could understand better that it is the "love of Christ that constrains us" (2 Cor. 5:14, paraphrased). An ongoing attitude of consecration is obviously essential if a person is to be able to pray effectively.

44

### Repentance

Another essential attitude in prayer is repentance. Much emphasis is given to God's forgiveness. Indeed, without His forgiveness we are lost. When God created the earth, He created oxygen before He created anything that would need it. In the same way He covered this earth with forgiveness before there was anyone who said "I'm sorry." We are kept alive not by breathing but by oxygen. However, the way we get oxygen is by breathing. In the same way we are kept alive spiritually not by repentance but by God's gracious forgiveness. Yet it is by repentance that His forgiveness is activated in our lives. This is why when we speak of the importance of the forgiveness of God, we should always at the same time point out the importance of repentance.

Repentance must always be accompanied by confession. It is strange how many are willing to confess but not to repent. Others say they have repented, but they are not willing to confess.

The Bible is clear that as we confess our faults to each other, we will be healed. If we continually wrong someone and don't confess it, the result will be a broken relationship. Nowhere is this more true than in marriage. If husbands and wives fight all the time, the situation will go from bad to worse if there is never any confession and asking for forgiveness.

Often when a couple is about to break up, one or the other will say, "Well, I never loved them anyhow." A person says this because at that point all they can remember are the many wrongs that were committed and never sincerely made right.

You may think, *Why bring it up again? It is over now. Why do I need to ask for forgiveness? The other person knows I'm sorry.* Friend, that can be a false assumption. The truth is the other person may not know or believe we are sorry. The wrong is filed away, and sooner or later it will come back to haunt the relationship, and will increase the pressure every time there is a falling out, until at last comes the final blowup that destroys the relationship.

When I was a little boy, we used to go barefoot most of the summer. Once in a while I stepped on a rusty nail. A rusty nail leaves a puncture wound. A puncture wound tends not to bleed. As you know, bleeding actually serves to clean a wound. So when I would step on a rusty nail, my parents made sure I got a tetanus shot.

When we wrong each other, even if it is by accident, the wound we leave must be cleansed. The Scripture says, "If we confess our sins, he is faithful and just to forgive us our sins, and to cleanse us from all unrighteousness" (1 John 1:9).

When we wound our spouse or family members, is not enough to think, *I know I was wrong, but I won't say anything; it will only make it worse.* Too many men in particular are afraid that if they admit they were wrong and ask for forgiveness, their families will lose respect for them. The reality is just the opposite. It is amazing how the carnal heart tries to avoid humbling itself and admitting it is wrong.

When we ask God to forgive our sins, we often say something like "Please forgive my sins." Or perhaps "Please forgive my sins and mistakes," or even "Lord, if I have committed any sins, please forgive me."

Passing through Jericho, Jesus was confronted by a blind man, who began to call out, "Jesus, thou son of David, have mercy on me" (Mark 10:47).

At first the people tried to keep him quiet. The blind man was embarrassing them. Jesus asked for the blind man to be brought forward. The man was led to Jesus by some friends. Then the Lord asked him a strange question: "What wilt thou that I should do unto thee?" (Mark 10:51). The first question that popped into my mind was *Lord, why are You asking him that? Isn't it obvious? Can't You see the man is blind?*

Here is a point that is basic to prayer. Prayer does not so much tell God what we need; He already knows what we need. Prayer is an admission of our need.

What does this have to do with asking God to forgive our sins? Everything! The inclination of the carnal heart is to avoid responsibility. Many times when we ask God to forgive our sins, we are saying in effect, "Lord, I know You are sensitive about sin. I recognize I am a sinner, but frankly, I would rather talk about something else. So if there is anything about me You think ought to be changed, please forgive it so that we can get on with our conversation."

Yet when we truly ask the Lord to forgive our sins, He has a question for us that we need to answer before we go on: "Which ones?"

There is a good reason for this. Often when we ask God to forgive our sins, we do not include all of them. Some we may not consider important; with others we know we are doing wrong, but we have our self-excusing reasons for hanging on to them.

One of the sins we often protect is that of temper. You probably know of people who have lost marriages, relationships with their children, and even their jobs because of temper. One person told me he had prayed and prayed about his temper but it didn't seem to do any good. But it turned out he was not bringing the entire problem of temper to God. How many times we ask Jesus to forgive our sins, but not all of them. Ninety percent, maybe! Who knows, you might need a little temper for a rainy day!

Someone might complain that I am trying to put them on a guilt trip by asking them to confess specific sins. They may think confessing generic sin would be all that is necessary. Friend, we need to put sin in its worst possible light. That is the only way we will ever get serious about it and let the Lord give us victory over it.

If you go to a doctor who says you have some common ailment that will go away in 24 hours, you are relaxed. If the doctor tells you what you have is life-threatening, your attitude is entirely different. Sins we hang on to are definitely life-threatening, and we need to put them in their worst possible light and take 100 percent of them to Jesus. Only then will we know the meaning of the promise that if we confess our sins, God is faithful and just to forgive us our sins and to cleanse us from all unrighteousness.

Our Saviour is a full-service Saviour. When we ask Him to forgive our sins, we must mean all our sins, each one. We are talking about pride, selfishness, bitterness, resentment, lust, the lack of self-control, and other mean little companions of our sinful lives.

When we have the true attitude of repentance and confession, it will bear real fruit in our lives. A person who is praying that the Lord

47

will forgive them of the same sin year in and year out needs to discover what is really wrong. A person who has let the Lord give them an attitude of confession and repentance will not be dominated by sin. The promise in Romans 6:14 is that sin will no longer have dominion over us.

An attitude of repentance accompanied by confession is probably the single most important component of the Christian life. We need to study how to overcome sin, but we need first to learn how to get out of sin once we fall into it. This knowledge will actually give us the key to becoming overcomers.

Obviously, when we talk about attitudes we can't help getting down deep into who we are and what we stand for. I may be over-simplifying it, but I believe our characters are to a large extent the sum of our attitudes.

This is why when we really begin to learn to understand what prayer is all about, we must address not just the things we do, but also our attitudes. It is a person's attitude that makes them do the things they do.

I don't know what the greatest burden of your prayers is at this moment, but I would suggest that if you are not already concerned about your attitudes, now is a good time to start. Don't worry about everybody else's attitudes; zero in on your own.

Understanding the priority of prayer teaches us that it is not something we do for God, but something God does for us. Prayer is the umbilical cord of the Christian life. In prayer the Christian life is sustained and nourished.

You might be wondering if you must have all these attitudes in the right amounts before your prayers will be effective; if so, you might feel like giving up right now, because you know you will never be able to attain all those attitudes.

Please, don't be discouraged and give up! The answer once again is in prayer. You see, prayer makes more prayer effective. Godly attitudes are a gift that the Lord has for us. But we must request them. Godly attitudes are what it means to *be* and as such are a priority of prayer.

### Doing a Reality Check

1. Think of the meaning of "We can rise no higher than our concept of God." What is your concept of God?

2. On a scale of 1 to 10, how would you rate your consecration to God?

3. How do you feel listening to sermons that call on you to repent?

4. Is there anyone close to you that you need to ask forgiveness of for something in the past or even for something that you may be doing against them right now?

### Fine-tuning Your Prayer Life

1. On the next clear night, look up at the stars or contemplate the greatness of God. Meditate on His goodness as you look at some of the photos sent back by the Hubble telescope.

2. Make sure that you have made a total commitment to Jesus.

3. Identify the most obvious sin in your life. Identify how it manifests itself. Ask God to make you sorry for it. Don't worry—the guilt that the Holy Spirit gives is a healthy guilt. When we follow 1 John 1:9, we are set free to actually know the meaning of being "cleansed from all unrighteousness."

### Prayer

Dear God: You made us and keep us. You are the only one that really matters. Without You our lives have no meaning. You are our Creator. You gave us our free will. We use our wills to commit our lives and all that we have to You.

We seem to sin so often. Help us to know when we are doing something that is not right and not to rationalize it, but to admit it. When we do this, You forgive us and make it possible for us to get back on the right road again.

Thank You for being the God of new beginnings.

Amen.

# Chapter 6

# More Essential Attitudes in Prayer

Our attitudes can make us do the things we do. We often miss this point and pray that God will change the things we do. The priority of prayer should be to change who we are. It is quite possible to do the right things and still have the wrong attitude. Someone with the right attitude will do right things from the heart. This is the reason that the priority of prayer is to *be*.

The promise is "A new heart also will I give you, and a new spirit will I put within you: and I will take away the stony heart out of your flesh, and I will give you an heart of flesh" (Eze. 36:26). But how does this new heart become ours? It comes through prayer, which has been called the opening of the heart to God. The new heart that the Lord puts in us has certain characteristics or attitudes.

### *Thanksgiving*

Usually when we talk about what we are thankful for, it has to do with material or physical things. And yes, we all have material and physical needs. There is nothing wrong with being thankful for these things. But if this is the sum of our thankfulness and for some reason we find ourselves out of work or have a serious illness, there go our blessings out the window!

I have worked in places in which the yearly income of the local people averaged $200 or less. Such is surely grinding poverty. Sometimes the offerings in church on Sabbath would amount to a fraction of a cent in our money, or perhaps an egg or a little pan of flour. Many people in this world literally live from hand to mouth and have nothing but the clothes on their backs. The Bible calls on the believer to be thankful. If being thankful depends on having material things, many Christians would not be able to comply.

Being thankful has a lot to do with expectations. A pastor friend of mine and I were once visiting in a home. He asked the woman of the house how her son was coming along. She explained that her son was studying for his examinations. I didn't know the young man they were talking about, but when it came time to leave, she asked, "Do you want to say goodbye to John?" So we went down the hall and into the first bedroom.

John was studying on the bed, propped on his elbows. I wondered why he hadn't come out to say hello to us, but I figured it was because he was busy. When he extended his hand to greet me, I saw that the hand was misshapen. At the same time I saw a wheelchair in the corner of the room. Then John explained to me that he was paralyzed from the chest down as the result of a diving accident.

As we talked, John said something that I have never forgotten: "I feel so sorry for people less fortunate than I."

*Less fortunate than you?* I thought. *Can't you see how unfortunate you are?* Of course I didn't say that, but I will never forget his words.

Thankfulness is an attitude that comes from expectations. Someone who thinks they deserve to be rich and famous will probably have few opportunities to be thankful.

Someone who imagines that if they are good enough they will be spared trouble and suffering is in for a big disappointment. Such a person will see little for which to thank God and will probably end up bitter and resentful.

Not long ago, as I was conducting some meetings, the door of the church opened and a woman in a wheelchair came in. She was severely disabled, and I could see she was controlling the chair with her teeth.

Later I said to her, with humor designed to underscore the reality of our faith, "I hope you know that when Jesus comes you are going to have to give up that wheelchair."

She responded, "I know." Then she declared, "Being in this wheelchair has taught me so much." I was amazed.

With an attitude of thanksgiving she was able to thank God for everything. She understood that God can bring good from whatever we may pass through in this life.

I don't know if you have realized it or not, but Jesus never promised us a bed of roses in this life. On the contrary, He said that in this world we would have big trouble, just as He did (John 16:33). Scripture is clear that suffering is the lot of the Christian (Rom. 8:17; 1 Thess. 3:4; 1 Peter 4:19).

We are told to expect suffering, yet in many other places in the New Testament we are called on to give thanks in everything. That surely means we are to be thankful even when we are going through suffering and trouble. This will be possible when we understand the meaning of the promise "All things work together for good to them that love God, to them who are the called according to his purpose" (Rom. 8:28).

For God to bring good from all that happens to us, we need to understand what things are really important. We need to have our priorities straight. If we think a big bank account is the ultimate experience and suddenly we lose all our savings, then what? As sons and daughters of God we must come to realize that "you can't take it with you"; and that includes not just our money but also our mortal bodies. We do take our character with us—and our character is the sum of our attitudes.

This means that by a miracle of His grace there is never a situation in which we are not developing our characters. Remember the text that says, "My brethren, count it all joy when ye fall into divers temptations [that means different kinds of trials]." It goes on to say, "Knowing this, that the trying of your faith worketh patience. But let patience have her perfect work, that ye may be perfect and entire, wanting in nothing" (James 1:2-4).

So an attitude of thankfulness is not built on sand castles; neither is it the denial of reality. It is a gift God gives us as a constant reminder that we are sons and daughters; He has forgiven our sins and is giving us a new heart (new attitudes).

I am not a sadist or a masochist. I do not enjoy suffering or seeing others suffer. However, I am a realist. This world of sin is about suffering. But in spite of it all, our God is in the process of saving us. Because of this we always, no matter what happens, have a reason to be thankful.

When you and I get to heaven, I'm sure that if someone were to ask me about some of the experiences I passed through here on earth, I would have to say that some of them were a nightmare. But I would also declare that I thank God forever. He shared His sorrow with me and through it all brought me near to Him. In my grief I have felt His love for me and have learned to love Him more. As God gives us an attitude of thankfulness, we will immediately notice how it affects our prayer life.

### Intercession

One of the most often referred to aspects of prayer is that which is called intercessory prayer. Many have even called it the epitome of prayer.

To intercede means to plead on another's behalf. In this regard I am sure that I am safe in saying we intercede in our prayers mostly for members of our family, especially for our children and our grandchildren. As you know, the devil is constantly encouraging our dear ones to sin. He tries to distract them from any and all influences that would draw them to the Lord.

Here is a prayer for them that we can pray at any time, and it will always be answered the moment we pray. It can go something like this: "Dear God, wherever [name of person] is at this moment, as the devil is trying to encourage them to stay away from You, I ask right now that You send angels that excel in power to push back the forces of evil and put Your thoughts in their mind."

A mother told me that shortly after she had begun offering this prayer on behalf of her son, she was talking to him on the phone and happened to speak to him about the shortness of time and the end of the world. He replied, "Mother, I was thinking about that yesterday!"

A person is more prone to turn to God for help in times of great distress than when all is well. Therefore, when we receive requests for prayer, be they for physical healing or material need, we need to expand our vision and include in our prayers of intercession those elements that seek first the kingdom of heaven and His righteousness.

One day a woman asked me to pray for her son. She said that he was not a believer and that he was out of work. She asked me to pray that he might find a job. I might have just prayed that the Lord would help the young man to find work. It was more consistent with the priority of prayer for me to pray first that God use this time of financial insecurity to cause the young man to think seriously about his spiritual condition; that through this distress he might come to know the Lord. Simply to pray that the young man find work, we might well be asking that the Lord remove an opportunity to bring salvation to the young man.

In the same way, when we are called upon to pray for the sick, we need to expand our intercession to include spiritual healing. Though sickness is a time of pain and distress in the family, it can be a time of spiritual healing, a realigning of life's priorities, and a time to make old wrongs right between family members. Simply to pray that God will take away the illness may well be to sell short His healing power for the sick person and those who are near and dear to them. Whether we are praying for the sick, for those in financial difficulty, or for those who are passing through some other of life's many problems, let us always remind ourselves to seek first for them the things that matter most.

Intercessory prayer begins to get more difficult when it includes praying for people we don't happen to be getting along with; or worse, the people we don't even like or with whom we happen to be angry. This is particularly true in the marriage relationship. It may be an oversimplification, but I suspect the divorce rate among Christians could be cut in half if one or the other of the spouses were to become an intercessor. The Bible insists we pray for one another (James 5:16). When a person stops praying because of problems with someone, there is not much hope for the relationship.

The current climate in this culture says that we don't have to put up with anything. Furthermore, if we value our self-esteem, we must not let people walk on us. This mind-set is making it nearly impossible to solve the problems we have among ourselves and to be effective intercessors for others.

It is natural to have problems. Whenever we have two people, there will be problems to be resolved. There have been problems in marriages since the very beginning. What is unique to this generation, however, is the apparent lack of will to give and take or to back down.

I don't know if you have ever lived in a country in which to shop requires bargaining. It is great fun to bargain. In Mexico a friend and I went buying souvenirs. My friend picked out something he liked. The owner of the shop told him how much he wanted for it. My friend offered half the amount. The shop owner came down 25 percent. My friend made another offer, more than half but less than what the owner wanted. Finally they reached a point where neither would give in. The disagreement amounted to about 50 cents!

I said to my friend, "Go ahead and give it to him."

My friend said, "No, that is my last price."

I said to the shop owner, "Go ahead and let him have it."

"No," said the owner, "that is my last price." Suddenly the shop owner said, "Let's flip for it; if you win, it is your price, if I win, it is mine." We all laughed, and my friend agreed. They flipped a coin, and the shop owner lost! But we all had a good laugh at the solution.

When two people must do business together, as in a marriage, someone is going to have to back down if they are to stay married. The problem with this selfish age is that we are being taught to "look out for number one" and to stand up for our rights and not let people put us down. With this kind of attitude it is impossible to stay happily married. The Scripture makes it clear when it asks, "Can two walk to-gether, except they be agreed?" (Amos 3:3). To live with others suc-cessfully, we must learn the art of backing down gracefully. Someone must become an intercessor. In this selfish age it is more and more difficult to find an intercessor, because a selfish person prays only for their own interests and for their selfish purposes.

The highest spirit of intercession is not my praying for me and mine, but rather an attitude that prays for those who disagree with me, even those who are taking advantage of me and using or abusing me.

The classic model of intercession is our Lord Jesus Christ. As they were nailing Him to the cross, He prayed, "Father, forgive them, for they know not what they do" (Luke 23:34).

"While we were yet sinners, Christ died for us" (Rom. 5:8). In an-other place Scripture says Jesus ever lives to make intercession for us (Heb. 7:25). All of this means intercession is an attitude that doesn't discriminate, not for race, color, creed, gender, or religion. Even more, it is an attitude that enables prayer for "enemies," who might actually be a person's husband or wife!

When we are bitter and resentful, we cannot be intercessors. This is because when we are bitter and resentful, we usually stop praying. And if we do continue to pray, our prayers tend to be spiritually gar-bled. Jesus may have told some parables that were hard to under-stand, but He wasn't talking in parables when He said if we don't forgive those who wrong us, He won't forgive us (Matt. 6:15). (The matter of bitterness and resentment is treated more fully in the chap-ters on barriers to answered prayer.)

Does all this sound tough and discouraging? Don't you think that if Jesus could create the heavens and the earth, if Jesus could heal the sick and raise the dead, He could certainly also give us a new heart and heal our bitterness, our resentment, and our anger?

The Bible commands us to love our enemies (Matt. 5:44). It de-clares that loving only our friends and the people who agree with us hardly has any value, because even the bad people love each other (Luke 6:32, 33). Jesus taught us that a person would be able to tell His followers by the attitude they show toward people who don't treat them well (verse 35).

The main point was that anybody can wish their friends well, but Jesus taught that you don't even have to be religious to do good to those who do good to you. That is only the "I'll scratch your back and you scratch mine" thing.

Those who are translated to heaven will sing the Song of Moses and the Lamb. I could not imagine what that song might be until I heard it explained that the Song of Moses and the Lamb is the song of those who have been intercessors. When God threatened to destroy the children of Israel for worshiping the golden calf, Moses interceded and told God that if He did that, He might as well blot his name also out of the book of life. What an example of intercession!

We often are the opposite of intercessors. We spend thousands to keep our sight; we spend thousands to save an arm or a leg. We even spend big money on our cars and houses. But how much effort do we expend as intercessors trying to save relationships, be they in the family, in the church, or with God?

The name "Satan" means adversary. He is our accuser. What a contrast to Jesus who lives to make intercession for us (Heb. 7:25)! Human nature being what it is, it is more natural for us to condemn each other than to intercede for one another. It is no wonder then that intercessory prayer is seen as prayer at its best!

### Doing a Reality Check

1. What is the first thing that comes to mind when something negative happens to you?

2. Think about why you don't like a certain person. What if God loved only those who loved Him?

### Fine-tuning Your Prayer Life

1. Identify something that is causing you grief at the present time. Write down something good that might come from it, then thank God for what He is going to do in your life through this experience.

2. Identify someone you don't like. Pray for them with the same spirit that you pray for someone who is dear to you. Afterward notice how it changes the way you feel toward them.

### Prayer

Lord, when we think about it, it seems that we complain more to You than we thank You. We are always asking You to get us out of something or other, rather than thanking You that You are able to help us become stronger, even when things are rough. When we have financial trouble, we often ask for more money instead of asking for forgiveness for covetousness. We ask You to heal our physical sicknesses more often than we ask You to heal our attitudes.

We are accustomed to praying for our loved ones and friends. But now we are going to do something new. In the spirit of Jesus, Lord, do for the heart of our enemy (put someone's name here) what we are asking You to do for our own hearts. Through the Holy Spirit, amen.

# Chapter 7

# The Key to Successful Prayer

We have become used to getting things done quickly and efficiently. We set clocks that turn on the oven. We set thermostats that automatically keep us warm or cool. In our cars we use cruise control. And even more amazing, commercial airliners have a computerized automatic pilot that can actually fly the plane.

However, this mentality of setting the timer, letting the computer do the job, or just pushing a button can very easily creep into our spiritual lives, especially our prayer lives.

Prayer can easily become mechanical and almost meaningless if we are not careful. I don't have to do a lot of thinking when I put on my socks in the morning. But if I begin to think I can pray the same way I put on my socks, sooner or later my prayer life will become just as perfunctory. The expression "no strings attached" is not true of prayer. Prayer definitely has strings attached.

Humility is a key to successful prayer, because a proud person doesn't especially feel the need for prayer. The word "humble" embraces lowliness of mind, lowly attitude, and a lowly estimate of oneself. It is the opposite of pride, conceit, arrogance, and haughtiness. It signals willingness to take a lowly place or to perform a lowly service.

Humility is not an "in" word these days. In a time when we hear so much about self-esteem and self-worth, it is important to understand the meaning of humility from a biblical perspective. The current emphasis on self-esteem and self-worth, if wrongly understood, can make humility impossible.

Something may be very valuable to me for personal or family reasons. It may be something that has been in the family for a long time, or something that invokes a lot of memories. But in monetary terms, its value is only what someone else is willing to pay me for the item.

I may say I have a piece of furniture that is worth $15,000. I may even have paid that much for it. Yet it is worth that amount of money only when I can find someone who will pay me what I paid.

A person can pay $25,000 for a new car, yet even as they drive it out of the showroom its value will have been considerably depreciated.

We were made in the image of God. Before sin came, we had value. After sin came, we lost that value. Our greed, selfishness, pride, and lack of self-control are not exactly what the unfallen beings and inhabitants of heaven would call collector's items. In fact, far from being of value, we actually represent a liability to the stability of the universe. But you would never know that to hear us talk. These days we have an aversion to people putting us down. We are constantly told, "You're a somebody" or "Don't let people walk on you." Pride and selfishness have been given legitimacy in our time and are often seen as something to be desired. In other generations it wasn't that way. Though pride and selfishness surely existed, they were seen as something to be avoided.

The Bible takes a dim view of the human race in its fallen condition. "Thou worm Jacob," it says in one place (Isa. 41:14). In another place it declares that our best can be compared with "filthy rags" (Isa. 64:6).

Jesus died to save us not because of who we are, but because of who He is. You remember the text "For God so loved the world, that he gave his only begotten Son, that whosoever believeth in him should not perish, but have everlasting life" (1 John 3:16). Notice it doesn't say whosoever believes in themselves, but whosoever believes in Him.

Our salvation is not about us; it is about God. This whole wonderful and terrible experience of life is not about our falling into a hill of fire ants and God in His love reaching down to pull us out. We actually became the fire ants. God reached down not to save His friends who had fallen on hard times, but to save those who had become His enemies. Romans 5:10 tells us Jesus died for us when we were His enemies. "For if, when we were enemies, we were reconciled to God by the death of his Son, much more, being reconciled, we shall be saved by his life."

A person who prays with the attitude that they deserve the best is like a serial killer saying to the judge, "I deserve a break." Jesus did not die by accident. It happened when a group of people who were proud, selfish, bitter and resentful, lustful, and without self-control suddenly realized their lifestyle and the way they did things was being threatened.

But were those who killed Jesus so different from me? I happen to know that deep down inside I am proud, selfish, bitter, lustful, and without self-control. But if we humans think this is simply being human and God is going to have to get used to it, please think again.

We like to say it was the priests and the rulers who killed Jesus: but really it was pride, selfishness, bitterness, lust, and the lack of self-control. Anyone who tries to justify these kinds of attitudes is out of touch with the truth, and if they persist in these attitudes, they declare themselves an enemy of God.

Yes, truly, humility must be a condition for prayer. If a person feels justified in being proud, selfish, bitter, lustful, and not having self-control, they probably shouldn't waste time praying, unless it be a prayer that the Lord will open their eyes to their need. The prayers that come from this mind-set might be classified among those that "don't go any higher than the ceiling."

This attitude even has trouble with the words of some hymns. For example: "Amazing grace, how sweet the sound, that saved a wretch like me." Many resent being called wretches. A pastor friend of mine told me of a prayer meeting at which the people formed a large circle, joined hands, and began to sing "Amazing Grace." He said that it was a beautiful experience. But when they had finished singing, someone spoke up and declared, "I'm not a wretch!"

By admitting we are wretches we are simply acknowledging that in our humanness we do not deserve the grace and love of God. This is because our attitudes are implicated in the murder of the Son of God.

Jesus made it clear that we must pray with the spirit of humility when He told the story of two men praying (Luke 18:11-13). One prayed, in effect, "God, I'm thankful I am not like the rest of this low-life." The other man prayed, "Lord, be merciful to me, a sinner." Jesus said that God heard that man's prayer rather than the prayer of the first.

Asking for the mercy of God is asking for healing, for a new heart. The mercy of God is not for sinners who like the way they are, but for sinners who want out of a sinful lifestyle and are willing to let the forgiveness of God put the past behind them.

It is written that Jesus associated with sinners, and indeed He did, but the sinners Jesus associated with were not content to stay in sin. They were the sinners who were fed up with selfishness, pride, lust, bitterness, and a lack of self-control. The sinners who followed Jesus were the ones who wanted out of sin. When they were with Jesus, they had hope, because it had been promised of the Messiah that He would save His people from their sins (Matt. 1:21).

There are two identifying marks of humility. The first is recognizing that I have problems I cannot solve and needs I cannot supply. The second identifying mark of humility, which must always accompany the first, is that the humble person will actually ask someone else for help.

My dad tells the story of a cousin who was so proud that if someone at the dinner table didn't offer her the mashed potatoes, she wouldn't ask for them. She was the type of person who wouldn't admit she needed anything, even to asking someone to pass her the potatoes!

When we understand what humility is, we will see why it is a key to successful prayer. The person who refuses to admit a need will not feel constrained to pray. This is because prayer is reaching outside oneself.

Jesus is the model for humility. He said, "Learn of me, for I am meek and lowly in heart" (Matt. 11:29). It is said of Him, "Being found in fashion as a man, he humbled himself, becoming obedient" (Phil. 2:8). He said, "I am among you as he that serveth" (Luke 22:27). Another time He said He "came not to be ministered unto, but to minister" (Matt. 20:28).

Humility is closely related to the grace of God. Someone who is not humble will not recognize their need of grace. Scripture says God "giveth grace to the humble" (1 Peter 5:5). Humbling ourselves is the key to receiving the grace of God. He cannot help a person who will not admit a sense of need.

We must take care as we consider the meaning of true humility. The person who is truly humble does not self-consciously feel humble or claim to be so. In other words, a person who claims to be humble isn't!

One day a little town decided to give a special award to the most humble person in town. They decided they would discover this individual by taking a door-to-door survey. It wasn't a very big town, so it would be easy to do.

They went door-to-door asking people who they considered the most humble person in town, then compiled the results. There was really no competition; one person was recognized by almost everyone in the town as being the most humble. So they arranged a special occasion at the local high school. The high school band would play several numbers, and the mayor would present the award.

The big day arrived. It was a wonderful ceremony. At last the honored person was called forward and presented with the award for being the most humble person in town. It was a fancy ribbon like those given out at the fair. It was inscribed "To the Most Humble Person in Town."

The people gave him a standing ovation, and the meeting was over. Unfortunately, the next day they had to take the award away from the fellow. He was actually wearing it!

### Doing a Reality Check

1. Humility is not often seen as a virtue today. We are admonished on all sides to "look out for number one" and to love ourselves

first. Are you willing to learn from Jesus the meaning of humility?

2. Are you willing to be humiliated? The only way a person can understand what it means to be humble is to be humiliated.

3. Is your self-worth something you get from yourself, or is it the worth Jesus has placed on you?

### Fine-tuning Your Prayer Life

1. Identify three specific ways you can put others first in your daily life.

2. Write a letter to God telling Him what you think it means to be humble.

Use Jesus as the model for humility. Use specific instances in His life in which He demonstrated humility and then make application to your own life. For example: "Lord, just as Jesus was humble when He . . . so in my life bring the same kind of humility when . . ."

### Prayer

Father, we are ashamed when we think of how we sometimes act. We tend to be proud and selfish without even trying. Your Son has called on us to learn to be meek and lowly as He is. We are not sure what this means. People around us declare we need to stick up for ourselves and love ourselves first. Lord, we almost fear to ask this, but please do what it takes to make us humble, as Jesus was. Thank You for Jesus. Amen.

# Chapter 8

# Praying in the Name of Jesus

Whell some people pray, they use the name of Jesus in almost every sentence, especially when the person praying is asking for a special favor. This might include a prayer to cast out evil spirits, a prayer for healing, or other prayers requesting a miracle.

The name of Jesus is seen by some as an almost magical word. Many believe the more often that name is used in a prayer, the more powerful the prayer will be.

This idea did not come out of thin air, but is based on some of the words of Jesus Himself.

"If ye shall ask any thing in my name, I will do it" (John 14:14).

"Ye have not chosen me, but I have chosen you, and ordained you, that ye should go and bring forth fruit, and that your fruit should remain: that whatsoever ye shall ask of the Father in my name, he may give it you" (John 15:16).

"And in that day ye shall ask me nothing. Verily, verily, I say unto you, Whatsoever ye shall ask the Father in my name, he will give it you" (John 16:23).

"Hitherto have ye asked nothing in my name: ask, and ye shall receive, that your joy may be full" (verse 24).

There are a number of texts that admonish us to pray in the name of Jesus. We need to have a clear understanding of what Jesus meant when He told us to pray in His name. Though these texts may appear to teach that the more often we pronounce the name of Jesus in our prayers the better, we must remind ourselves of the counsel Jesus gives us in Matthew 6:7: "When ye pray, use not vain repetitions, as the heathen do: for they think that they shall be heard for their much speaking."

Even today many are as superstitious as the sick people who waited by the Pool of Bethesda in the days of Jesus. Folklore had it that when the water in the pool became agitated by what was thought to be an angel, the first person in would be healed. If a person managed to get into the pool and wasn't healed, they would say it was probably because someone got in ahead of them. Superstitious people often make excuses when their superstitions don't seem to work.

We get excited when we hear stories about answers to prayer, because just like the sick people lying around the pool we all have problems in our lives we would like to get rid of. When we don't seem to be getting answers, we begin to wonder if we are using the right words or if we are invoking them often enough or in the right order.

One day a woman asked me what the secret to answered prayer was. She said her prayers didn't seem to be working. She wanted to know to whom we should pray, the Father, the Son, or the Holy Spirit. Since nothing was happening as a result of her prayers, she figured she must be praying to the wrong Person!

What did Jesus mean when He told us to pray in His name? Is it simply a matter of saying His name in just the right places in our prayers? What does it mean to pray in the name of Jesus?

Let us suppose a certain person has been appointed development officer for Southern Adventist University. Their primary responsibility is to raise money for the institution. The relationship of the development officer to the university and how they represent that institution to the public might help us understand what it means to pray in the name of Jesus.

1. In the first place, this person has been authorized to do business for the institution. The university administration gives them the authority to represent them in an official capacity.

66

2. This means the person will be doing business on behalf of the school and not for themselves.

3. They must do what the university has authorized them to do on its behalf. The development officer does not decide for themselves what the school wants them to do. The administration will give them specific projects and the guidelines to use in the project.

4. The representative must make contacts on behalf of the university, according to its purposes and programs and for its benefits and not their own. When they collect money, they must turn it over to the school administration and not put it in their own pocket. If they were to do that, it would be fraud.

5. Finally, any benefits, profits, or glory resulting from their work in the name of the university do not belong to them, but to the university.

So, in summary, the development officer is authorized by the university, directed by the university, supported by the university, and rewarded by the university.

When we pray in the name of Jesus, we must pray by His authorization, which of course He has given. We must let Him guide us through His Word. Our prayers must be for His sake and for the progress of His work.

Understanding the significance of this, we see that praying in the name of Jesus rules out all selfish praying. It also excludes all careless praying and all ignorant praying. Praying in the name of Jesus does not mean saying whatever pops into our heads, either, although it is important that we allow the Holy Spirit to lead us in our prayers. Before we pray we would do well to think about what we are going to be praying about.

To pray in the name of Jesus is to pray thoughtfully. Have you noticed that we sometimes get into the habit of praying like this: "Shall we bow our heads for a word of prayer our Father we thank Thee for . . ." or "Before you go let's have a word of prayer dear heavenly Father we are so thankful . . ." These are not typing mistakes. They are written as we sometimes say them—quickly and all in one breath. In general we might do well to pause a moment or two after we bow our heads before we begin to pray. That moment or two gives us time to prepare our hearts and not be so prone to improvise and repeat ourselves as we proceed to pray.

To pray in the name of Jesus means that we will pray for His kingdom to come and His will to be done on earth as it is in heaven. And when we make specific requests to Him in prayer, we will consider how our requests fit into the larger picture of doing His will and bringing glory to His name. There is no such thing as a neutral prayer. Our prayers are either in His interest, that is, to His glory, or they are prompted by our own interests and desires.

Not long ago I was in a prayer group in which there were requests for special prayer. When a person made a request, another of the group asked if someone would agree with the request. When someone said they would agree, then the prayer was offered. They were applying Matthew 18:19 quite literally: "If two of you shall agree on earth as touching any thing that they shall ask, it shall be done for them of my Father which is in heaven." To pray in the name of Jesus means more than our agreeing together when we pray: it means that we should be concerned that our mutual requests agree more with His will than with ours!

As you read this you might be thinking to yourself, *I was hoping that reading this book would speed up my prayer life. But you seem to be slowing it down.*

This is not my purpose. Prayer is much more serious to God than it has been to us. How thankful I am that He is patient. He does not wait to hear our prayers until we pray perfectly. Just as proud parents are so excited to hear the first lisped words of their baby, so our heavenly Father takes joy in our lisped and imperfect prayers. But just as a child grows in vocabulary and in pronunciation, so we are to grow in prayer. As we grow better able to communicate with our heavenly Parent, He is better able to communicate to us an understanding of His Word—which is His will.

I hope that you have seen in this chapter the great truth that praying in the name of Jesus is not about saying His name as often as possible in our prayers. It is making sure that our prayers are consistent with all that He stands for and that He wants us to be.

### Doing a Reality Check

1. Can you recognize times in which your prayers were more likely to develop your own kingdom than the kingdom of God?

2. What does a selfish prayer look like?

### Fine-tuning Your Prayer Life

1. The next time someone asks you to pray, instead of beginning immediately, pause a few moments and contemplate what you want to say. This pause will capture the thoughts of those who are with you and focus them on the prayer to come.

2. Make a list of the things you have been praying about lately. Determine if they fit the criteria of being: (1) authorized by Christ, (2) for His sake, (3) essential for His work, (4) consistent with His Word, and (5) for His glory.

### Prayer

Our Father and Father of Jesus Christ, what a wonderful thing it is to talk to You and know that You hear every word. You don't have any trouble understanding us, but we do not always understand You. You know what we really need, but sometimes we don't know or won't admit our own needs.

We know Jesus is willing to use His power to do for us what needs to be done. We want our prayers to represent not only our feelings, but His feelings; not just our plans, but His also. We are eager to give Him all the praise, the honor, and the glory. Amen.

# Chapter 9

# Praying in the Spirit

In recent years the Christian world has shown a great interest in the subject of the Holy Spirit. Many books are being written about the Spirit, and Christians everywhere are admonished to pray for and receive the blessing of His presence. Interest in the Holy Spirit is so great that when you visit some churches you are likely to hear more about the Holy Spirit than about Jesus.

This chapter does not attempt to be a comprehensive study of the Holy Spirit. It addresses the subject primarily as it pertains to the focus of prayer. Yes, we should pray in the Spirit. But what does that mean, and what should our prayers be like when we are praying in the Spirit? For us to pray in the Spirit presupposes that we must have evidence of the Spirit being manifested in our lives.

A few years ago I abandoned my prejudice and learned how to use a computer. I had to convince myself that I could actually type and make up a sermon at the same time. I found out that I could, and I have come to enjoy it.

One day, while browsing through some of the resources available on America Online, I clicked on the religion section and then specifically on "Christianity." From there I discovered a religious forum. A forum is a place where people who have usually never met each other carry on typed conversations. In this instance the forum was set up to discuss spiritual issues.

Entering the forum, I noticed that someone had left a question addressed to "Anyone." The question was about sanctification. The person wanted to know what John Wesley and Charles Finney had taught about salvation (John Wesley was the founder of the Methodist Church, and Charles Finney was a lawyer in the past century who became a revivalist).

In answer to the question someone else had left a message: "I've been saved now for a number of years and I speak in tongues. What do you want to know?"

I was interested by the words "I speak in tongues." I know what the person meant. He was saying that because he spoke in tongues, he believed he had the Holy Spirit, and as such he could be trusted to give the right answer to religious questions.

What is called the "gift of tongues" is seen by many as indisputable evidence that a person has the Holy Spirit. The Bible teaches us that the Spirit gives gifts to the church, and we must realize that He does many other things for us besides the bestowing of this particular gift, however it might be defined. Scripture is clear, also, on what the Holy Spirit does in the life and the sequence in which His work is done (John 16:7-11).

In some table games, if a person gets a certain number card or has a high number spin, they are able to advance by skipping several spaces rather than only one space at a time. This doesn't happen in spiritual matters. There is a certain order of events, and there are no exceptions. For instance, when we plant a seed, we don't expect to pick a flower until a certain number of other things have happened first. Some people see the Holy Spirit as an exception to this rule. He is often seen as a marvelous supermarket where a Christian can walk along the aisles and say, "I'll take a little of this and some of that."

The first thing the Holy Spirit does is convict a person of sin (John 16:8). An ongoing spirit of repentance, confession, and forsaking of sin is the first evidence that a person has the presence of the Holy Spirit in their lives. If this is not evident, the Spirit is not present.

Second, a person who has the Holy Spirit will earnestly desire the righteousness of Jesus. As the Scripture says, they will "hunger and thirst after righteousness" (Matt. 5:6). This is because the Spirit, after He convicts of sin, convicts of righteousness. This results in what the Scriptures call the fruit of the Spirit (Gal. 5:22, 23). A person who has the Holy Spirit will begin to exhibit true love. They will be easier to get along with and will become patient and gentle. They will desire with all their hearts to be good, faithful, and humble, and they will pray for self-control.

There is a perception that the Holy Spirit manifests Himself in jumping, clapping, shouting "Amen," or falling on the floor. In recent years there has been a manifestation of what is called "holy laughter." But we should be cautious before we say this is unmistakably the work of the Holy Ghost.

A minister friend of another faith told me it used to confuse him when he saw people who were living together without being married claiming to have the gift of speaking in tongues. Can you see the dilemma? How can the Holy Spirit, whose first work is to convict the world that adulterers and fornicators cannot be saved unless they repent of their immoral lifestyles, proceed to say, "Never mind those details. Let Me give these people a miraculous gift." My friend, this could never happen (Mark 3:22-26).

Praying in the Holy Spirit does not necessarily mean being noisy. A person who prays in the Holy Spirit is more likely to be quiet. A person who prays in the Holy Spirit will more often be found with tears than shouting or jumping.

The Holy Spirit works way down deep at the level of the spirit of the human being. That is at the level of who we are. Remember when Elijah met God in the mountain? God first sent a huge wind and later an awesome fire. The Scriptures say that God was not in the wind or the fire. He revealed Himself in a still, small voice (1 Kings 19:12).

If you really want to hear the voice of the Holy Spirit, you don't want to get loud, but quiet. In fact, it is the dark forces that use noise to get things worked up for them. Often the devil uses drum rhythms to prepare people to do things that they would not otherwise do.

We know how to be carnal and we know how to be sensual, but we don't naturally know how to be spiritually intimate with God. In human relationships intimacy is often the road to sensuality (the dictionary meaning being erotic desire or sexual appetite). But being intimate with God will not manifest itself in sensual feelings or expressions. Jesus said those who would truly be intimate with God would be so on the level of the Spirit. He said those who worship God must do so in spirit and in truth (John 4:24).

By nature humans know how to be sensually intimate, but they do not know naturally how to be spiritually intimate. That is something the Spirit must teach or, better said, something that He must lead us into through a work He does deep down at the level of who we are.

What part does the Holy Spirit have in the matter of prayer? Scripture says we don't know how to pray as we should. It is the Holy Spirit that teaches us (Rom. 8:26, 27). To invite the Spirit to pray with us or teach us to pray means we will pray at the level of total surrender of ourselves to God.

If the first work of the Holy Spirit is to convict of sin, a person who is not sincerely responding to that work might be opening themselves up to another spirit—a spirit of error and deception—if they are only seeking some kind of physical manifestation. The following verses from 2 Thessalonians 2:9-12 are very relevant to this: "Even him, whose coming is after the working of Satan with all power and signs and lying wonders, and with all deceivableness of unrighteousness in them that perish; because they received not the love of the truth, that they might be saved And for this cause God shall send them strong delusion, that they should believe a lie: that they all might be damned who believed not the truth, but had pleasure in unrighteousness."

Resisting the sequential ministry of the Holy Spirit is not a thing to be taken lightly! This passage is telling us that to do so is to open ourselves up to delusions that could cause us to be lost.

If we really wish to learn to pray, we must ask God for the Holy Spirit, for the Spirit alone can teach us how to pray as we ought (John 16:13).

God has promised to give the indwelling, internal Holy Spirit. Internal refers to the level of a person's being or what they are down deep inside. The Holy Spirit teaches, brings things to mind, and convicts of sin. He gives the fruit of the Spirit. He gives insight and understanding of the truth, of faith, and of victory over sin. All these things are intensely personal. They are the very essence and life of who we are. And, of course, the Spirit also gives gifts for the edifying of the church.

Someone might say, "But I know people who say they are sure they have the Holy Spirit." We must be careful. The Scripture says we should not believe every spirit, but try the spirits, whether they are of God (1 John 4:1). A woman wrote me affirming that the true test of having the Holy Spirit is speaking in tongues. She told me she was able to discern who was true and who was false, because God revealed it to her heart.

Have you ever been cutting boards to a specific length and used the last one cut as the measure to cut the next one? You know what happens: the boards keep getting shorter and shorter. Just so, we must not trust our own hearts in determining matters of the Word of God.

A person who thinks the Holy Spirit is primarily about some specific physical manifestation is setting themselves up for problems. Worse, they will miss the point of what the deeper work of the Holy Spirit is all about.

Praying in the Spirit is praying to *be;* in a miraculous way that we don't understand, the Holy Spirit will graft the spirit of the crucified and risen Saviour into our hearts (John 3:6-8).

### Doing a Reality Check

1. Is it possible that a person may want to possess the Holy Spirit and yet resist the work of the Spirit in the life?

2. Do you see a danger in seeking physical manifestations as a sign of the Holy Spirit? Could a person have certain physical manifestations and not have the Holy Spirit at all?

3. When you are under the deepest conviction of sin, how will you be inclined to express it externally?

4. Are you willing for the Holy Spirit to work in your life, convicting you of sin, of righteousness, and of judgment?

### *Fine-tuning Your Prayer Life*

1. Pray that the Holy Spirit will make you sensitive to sin. How will this change some things in your life?

2. Pray that the Holy Spirit will manifest His presence by giving you the fruit of the Spirit. How will things be different than they are now?

3. If someone asks you if you pray in the Spirit, how will you explain to them that you do?

### *Prayer*

Dear Jesus, thank You for not leaving us alone when You returned to heaven. You followed through on Your promise to send the Holy Spirit as a down payment on the salvation You purchased for us.

Lord, we know there are more things in store for us than we can even imagine. Your Word has said we can't even imagine all the good things You have for us. But we see the need to put first things first. We want the fruit of the Spirit in our lives as a prerequisite to whatever other gifts You might have in store.

Jesus, go ahead and finish the good work You have begun through Your Spirit in our hearts. Amen.

# Chapter 10

# The Role of
# Meditation in Prayer

Prayer is not for God's benefit, but for ours. God speaks all languages and can read every heart. Before we even begin to pray, God knows our need. Our greatest challenge is not getting through to God, but permitting Him to get through to us.

Sin has clouded our thinking. It has clouded even our subconscious to the point that we have a mental block when it comes to spiritual things. We have all heard of people who after a head injury have to relearn the things they once did naturally. Something like this has happened to our race. Scripture says, "Your iniquities have separated between you and your God" (Isa. 59:2). Although God is still there, we have lost the ability to communicate with Him effectively.

Many years ago my dad was introduced to a young man and woman. After they had left, he was informed that the couple were married but not living together. The young wife had undergone brain surgery and as a result had forgotten her past. That included memory of her husband. The doctor told the young man not to worry, but to bring in the marriage certificate and show it to her. Surely that would convince her they were married. But even when she saw the marriage certificate, she refused to move back in with her husband.

She said, "How can I live with you as my husband if I don't know you?" However, she agreed to let him court her again, and fortunately she fell in love with him all over again.

That story illustrates what sin has done to us. God created us to love Him. He has never ceased to love us. It is we who have ceased to love and even ceased to know Him. His Word declares we were made by Him (John 1:3), but that doesn't seem to change our feelings about Him automatically. In a way, we could say that salvation is the process by which God is courting us, trying to win us back to Him.

Prayer is communicating with God. For communication to be effective it must be two-way. As a ham radio operator, I know that a piece of shortwave equipment, if it is going to be complete, has to have not only a transmitter but a receiver. If our communication with God is to be complete, we must learn not only to express ourselves to Him but also learn how He expresses Himself to us.

Meditation is a word often used in conjunction with prayer. Knowing what meditation is and how it functions is an essential component of knowing how to pray effectively.

It is common to control day-to-day finances through a checking account. A checking account allows us to transfer funds from our account to someone else's account. Of course, to do this we must already have money in our account.

We continually have to monitor the amount of money we are taking out of the account to make sure we have enough to cover the checks we write. It is no fun to get a notice from the bank advising us that they have charged us $20 for writing a check with insufficient funds.

The problem is even more complicated if you run a business. There is the matter of employee payrolls, withholding taxes, and so on. How you maintain your accounts will decide whether or not you stay in business.

We spend time and effort to keep things going in our businesses and professions. We maintain accurate records. There are audits and reviews to endure. We do all this to ensure that the business will succeed.

Of course, it goes further than making sure our finances are in good shape. We have to be continually keeping our real property maintained and in good repair and secure.

We go to great effort trying to keep everything together in the financial and material aspects of our lives. We have health insurance and physical checkups. We take vitamins and supplements. If there is some problem, we make an appointment with the doctor. If the doctor prescribes that we take a certain medication every day, we do it, and when the prescription is about to run out, we call in for a renewal.

But in the area of our lives that really matters, many of us don't give a second thought to what is happening. We may well be aware that things are not going well in our spiritual lives, but we will do little about it. This is not benign neglect; this is fatal neglect. It is something that we would never let happen if we developed a suspicious lump on a part of our bodies, or if we started getting notices from the bank that our checks were bouncing, or if in our business we hadn't had any customers in six months.

Many are serious about every area of their lives except their relationship with God—the area that really matters. We don't think it unusual to have to keep the house clean, or do preventive maintenance on the car, or keep the checkbook balanced. It shouldn't seem unusual then that we should have to keep track of how things are going in our spiritual lives as well. This is done through meditation.

Meditation is that part of prayer in which we take the Bible—which is God speaking to us—and apply it to the real and practical aspects of our everyday lives. The time of meditation is when in our minds we make practical application of the Word of God to our own experience.

Meditation is like keeping the spiritual checkbook balanced. It is changing the oil in the vehicle of life. Learning the meaning of meditation goes a long way toward keeping us out of spiritual trouble. Many are driving their spiritual lives with their eyes shut and having some tremendous wrecks as a result. You could say that it is through meditation that we are able to see where we are going in the Christian life. Meditation is the process by which we discover where and why we went off the road spiritually. It is also a vital part of the process that gets us back on the road.

If running a successful business is no accident, if keeping the house in good repair is no accident, if getting a prescription for antibiotics is no accident, then neither is staying on the spiritual road something that just happens. A meaningful and growing commitment to the Lord doesn't come naturally.

Meditation in the scriptural sense of the word is not sitting cross-legged or standing on your head with arms folded and a faraway look in the eye. Meditation is not passive; it is active. It is not something that happens to us; it is something we initiate. The psalmist David said he meditated on the law of the Lord day and night (Ps. 1:2). To him meditating on the law of the Lord meant thinking about the Word of God. It meant he was continually testing and checking his life to see if it was in line with the will of God.

One of the texts that says it best is Joshua 1:8: "This book of the law shall not depart out of thy mouth; but thou shalt meditate therein day and night, that thou mayest observe to do according to all that is written therein: for then thou shalt make thy way prosperous, and then thou shalt have good success."

A person must not only read the Bible, but must also continually make application of what it is saying to the everyday life. Otherwise the Bible can be considered just another interesting book.

Meditation and prayer go together. On one hand we read God's Word. That is His speaking to us. Then we meditate on what we have read, to make practical application of those principles in our own lives. When we have done this, then we can open our hearts to Him in prayer and pray that He will remove from us everything that would stand in the way of implementing His will in our lives. And then in a wonderful and mysterious way the Holy Spirit makes it happen.

Let's look at a typical way meditation might work. During our morning devotions we read the passage in John 13:14, 15 in which Jesus says, "If I then, your Lord and Master, have washed your feet; ye also ought to wash one another's feet. For I have given you an example, that ye should do as I have done to you."

After reading this we ask ourselves the question "How would this be applicable to my life?" Perhaps we often feel that people are trying to take advantage of us, and we resent it. But this text reminds us that the Creator of heaven and earth came with the one purpose of helping others—and He tells us that we must do the same.

First we read the text. Next we apply it to our own lives. Then we ask the Lord to forgive us for "growing weary in well doing." We thank Him for His life of service, and we ask Him for the grace and strength to serve without complaining.

This illustration of how meditating makes the Word real may touch a sensitive chord in some; but that is what meditation and prayer are supposed to do! When we stop praying in generalities and begin to make specific applications of the Word of God to our lives, then our lives become dramatically different. This is what it means to pray to *be!*

Preventive maintenance keeps our cars running smoothly. I hope that you can see now that meditation and prayer are the preventive maintenance of the Christian life. If we would only take our relationship with God half as seriously as we do our relationship with the credit card company or the bank, our lives would not be in such difficulty and trouble.

Just as a cashier has to cash in on coming to work and cash out on leaving, we should cash in with God in the morning and then cash out with Him before we go to sleep at night. At night we should go through all that has happened to us throughout the day— the good, the bad, and the ugly. We will then discover how our lives were or were not in relationship to His Word. Then we will be able to pray intelligently to Him before we lie down to sleep.

So, then, meditation is not sitting staring into space. Meditation is not passive but active. It is the application of the Word of God to our hearts and lives. Meditation is what gives meaning and relevance to our prayers.

### Doing a Reality Check

1. When you read the Bible, do you make direct applications of what you read to your own life? (The tendency can be to apply it to other people!)

2. At the end of the day do you cash out with God (think about whether your life during the day was in right relationship to His Word)?

### *Fine-tuning Your Prayer Life*

1. Read 1 Corinthians 13:4. This verse tells what love is like. Take just two qualities—patient and kind. Write down specific ways you need to be patient in your daily life. What are the environments that make you impatient? Contemplate what it means to be kind. To whom do you especially need to be kind?

2. Ask God to help you remember to apply your resolve and give you the grace to put it into practice.

### *Prayer*

Our Father, the challenge of our lives is enormous. However, You have given it to us in pieces—minutes, hours, days. Please forgive us for being more particular about keeping our checkbooks balanced than in keeping our lives in balance with You.

We recognize there are many problems that come as a result of our not cashing in with You in the morning and cashing out at the end of the day. Your Word is a lamp unto our feet and a light unto our path, but we often don't pay much attention to it until we hit the wall or run off the road.

We forget so easily because of all the cares of this life. Lord, remind us throughout the day to keep the light of Your Word. Thank You for being so patient with us! We can't wait to be with You in person. Amen.

# Chapter 11

# How to Pray Without Ceasing

The Scripture calls on us to pray without ceasing. But does this mean we should be praying every minute of every day? That would seem impossible. To pray without ceasing means to not give up on prayer.

Jesus illustrated this in the story of the widow and an unjust judge (Luke 18:17). At first reading it seems to be teaching that God does not want to answer prayer and that we must nag in order for Him to respond. But this is not the point at all.

In the parable the woman needs to have a wrong made right. Someone is taking advantage of her. She is asking that the judge "avenge her." In today's language, she needed the judge to put a restraining order on the people who were making life hard for her, or for him to require them to pay monetary damages. The woman was appealing for justice. Apparently the judge wasn't doing anything about her problem.

On one level Jesus is saying that if even a corrupt judge will finally give in and help a person persistently asking for help, how much more will our heavenly Father be willing and eager to do what is best for us.

Another point, perhaps the most important as far as our prayers are concerned, is that the woman didn't give up asking. To use a modern term, she continued to appeal the case. She didn't accept the unacceptable. She persisted in her appeal to the judge until justice was done. This speaks to us and what it means to pray without ceasing.

This world is so full of pain and suffering that it is hard to stay sensitive to it all. We tend to develop emotional calluses to much of what is going on in order to protect ourselves. But this tendency to become emotionally and spiritually calloused can work against us, especially in the matter of prayer.

Most of us know someone who has left the Lord. We carry a concern for them in our hearts and pray for their conversion. However, it is possible to become tired of praying for them. Of course we do continue to pray, but maybe not with all the feelings we once had when they first fell away.

A backslider once declared to me that his mother and father should accept him the way he was and stop hoping he would change. With tears in my eyes I told him his parents would always love him but could never accept his unsaved condition. When I assured him that his mother and father would not cease to pray until he had returned to the Lord, he too had tears in his eyes.

Scripture calls us to persistent, tireless prayer. Just because nothing happens at once doesn't mean God is denying our prayers. It sometimes takes time to get into trouble, and it sometimes takes time—sometimes years—to get out.

In many cases the devil has quite successfully interrupted the saints' prayers of intercession. He causes them to become so accustomed to the way things are that many simply give up. They seem to have accepted the abnormal as normal. They have chosen to accept the best of the worst. The unacceptable has somehow now become acceptable.

To pray without ceasing means we must be willing to continue to suffer. We must be willing to continue to cry. We cannot become desensitized to the state of the lost or to the sin that surrounds us on every side. Sometimes we wish we didn't have to look anymore. We wish we could wake up one day and it would all be gone. But, my friends, that cannot be yet. Jesus, our example, was a man of sorrows and acquainted with grief. He foresaw that in this world we would have tribulation, sorrow, and suffering (John 16:33). But in our suffering we must continue to plead with the Lord day and night for deliverance for ourselves and our loved ones.

If we don't plead anymore, it can mean we have ceased to notice, we have accepted the unacceptable. Perhaps worse yet, we may ourselves have caught the spiritual disease we were praying about in the life of one of our loved ones. These days leprosy is called Hansen's disease. Leprosy affects the ability to feel pain. A person with leprosy won't feel it if they get burned. They sense no pain if a finger becomes infected. A leper can slam their hand in a car door and feel nothing, so they will have no incentive to treat it for the break or tissue damage.

Pain is necessary in this world of accident and sin. Pain is actually a safeguard to protect us from destroying ourselves. Our tendency is to try to turn off the pain in our lives. But we should first be interested in finding out what is causing it. Pain is a warning that something is wrong.

To pray without ceasing, we must be in pain. We must feel compassion and sorrow, both for the condition of others and for our own condition. Sometimes we get tired of praying; we want to get on with our lives. But the Scripture says Jesus lives *ever* to make intercession for us; and as long as God shall give us breath, we are called to pray and make intercession for others.

There is another element to persistent prayer. Imagine what would happen if the instant we prayed God always did what we asked? This could be dangerous for our spiritual lives and our relationship with Him. Remember, we do not know how to pray as we ought to. We are by nature selfish. The Scripture says we tend to pray for selfish reasons (James 4:3). We can even be praying for the right things for very wrong reasons.

If God were to answer all our prayers in an instant, it would begin to give us the idea that we were in charge and not He. The expression "When I say frog, you jump" would characterize our relationship to God. Prayer is not to get God to do our will, but to bring us to accepting His.

Some subscribe to the idea "Name it and claim it." This attitude tends to use faith as a force against God's will. Such people maintain you can receive if you pray and have enough faith. But this is not what prayer is about. Results from using this presumptuous prayer strategy may not be from God at all, but possibly "blessings" from the dark side.

It is well to remember that just because a person prays for something and it happens does not mean God answered the prayer. Scripture says that in the last days the devil will perform signs and wonders. What more effective way of getting people to do his will than for him to take over their prayer life? (This will be discussed more fully in the chapter "The Devil Also Answers Prayer.")

If you are experiencing what seems to be a delay in the answer to your prayers, don't give up or think God does not hear or does not care. Rather, we should see the delay as something that may take some time ("God's purposes know no haste and no delay" [*The Desire of Ages*, p. 32]). Or perhaps there is something God needs to do in our own lives before He can work effectively in the lives of those for whom we are praying.

Answering prayer is God's business. Yours and mine is to continue to pray—to pray without ceasing. Our marching orders are to pray and not give up.

### Doing a Reality Check

1. Are you discouraged about praying for someone on your heart? Have your prayers for that person become mechanical through the years and perhaps lost some fervor?

2. Have you given up praying for anyone?

3. If you had abundant money, were healthy and strong, and all your loved ones were active in Christian service, what would you be praying about?

### Fine-tuning Your Prayer Life

1. Thank Jesus for never giving up on you. Ask Him to forgive you

when you get tired of praying. Ask Him for the strength to continue.

2. As you pray for someone the Lord has laid on your heart, examine your own life to see if there is anything that could be a stumbling block, keeping that person from returning to the Lord. Is your relationship with that person consistent with your prayers for them?

3. Ask the Lord to give you the courage to make anything right that needs to be made right. "The effectual, fervent prayer of a righteous man availeth much" (James 5:16). The Lord wants to be able to use us to answer our own prayers!

### *Prayer*

Holy Father, we have many things on our hearts. You know what they are. Thank You for giving us families and children. But many of us have children and family members who have left You or have never given their hearts to You. We have brought their names to You many times; in fact, in every prayer we pray.

If only our loved ones would give their hearts to You. Then our burden would be lifted. There are times we wonder if they will ever come to You. Sometimes we are so discouraged we feel we can't look anymore.

You have been so patient with us, and You have never given up on us. Please give us the strength to keep interceding for others. We pledge to be faithful intercessors and pray for them while they are not praying for themselves. We know You love them more than we do. We know You always hear our prayers. In Jesus' name we pray, amen.

# Chapter 12

# Prayer and Natural Law

There is a story of a certain man caught in a flood. The waters were rising all around his house. Since he couldn't bring himself to believe that water would really overflow the house, he didn't leave. But the water continued to rise, and so he climbed up on the roof. The man was a religious person, and as the water continued to rise, he began to pray the Lord would save him.

About this time a boat came along, and the people in the boat said, "Get in. We'll get you out of here."

"I'm not going with you," said the man. "The Lord will save me."

The water continued to rise, and the man continued to pray that God would save him. Just as the water reached to the peak of the roof where the man was sitting, a helicopter flew over and let down a basket to haul him up. The man waved them off, shouting, "Don't worry about me. The Lord is going to save me."

The water continued to rise, and the man was swept away. When the man arrived in heaven, the Lord met him there. He was upset and asked, "Lord, I prayed You would save me. Why did You let me drown? Why didn't You answer my prayer?"

The Lord responded, "I tried to save you two times. I sent a boat and a helicopter." (Please note that this is not a story about the state of the dead!)

In Matthew 7:7 Jesus gives us some details about prayer. He said,

"Ask, and it shall be given you; seek, and ye shall find; knock, and it shall be opened unto you." This text should not be taken lightly. It tells us how prayer works and how we must cooperate with God in prayer.

Sometimes we consider the superstitious to be unenlightened. But many of us border on the irrational—at least the presumptuous—when it comes to the matter of prayer. The story of the man in the flood perfectly illustrates the prayer attitudes of some.

Could it be we see prayer as something in the realm of magic? Might praying be what we do when all else has failed, or something we engage in to get out of having to do anything ourselves—something practical, such as climbing into a boat or getting on board a helicopter?

There seem to be two extremes. One extreme is expressed in the philosophy "The Lord helps those who help themselves." We have heard this saying for so long that some attribute it to the Bible, but this is not so. It most likely comes from the philosophy of Aesop. Of course, it all but takes away the necessity for prayer if we can do it all ourselves.

The other extreme is illustrated by the man on the roof in the flood. Such people pray the Lord will solve the problem by waving a magic wand.

Have you considered that what we call the laws of nature, or natural law, or Mother Nature are all really the laws of God? What we call the law of physics is in reality the law of God. The laws of health are the laws of God. These laws that work from cause to effect have been established by God as the way things will be.

Then whatever cuts across the way things were meant to be is going to be a problem for us. We have already seen that the purpose of prayer is to understand the will of God, and then to ask Him for the strength to implement His will in our lives and in the lives of those we love. We could now say it another way: the purpose of prayer is to understand the laws of God and to ask Him to give us the strength to obey them. The concepts are essentially the same.

Whether we realize it or not, we are at the mercy of our heavenly Father's laws in every aspect of our lives. Even the people who don't believe in God are the beneficiaries of His laws. In the first place, our very existence is His doing. We breathe, we eat, we live, and we move by His will (Acts 17:28). All this is made possible by a force outside ourselves, and this power is the power of God. This power is expressed in His laws.

We do not create food; we merely raise it. We do not make seeds; we only plant them. We breathe oxygen, yet we don't decide to breathe—our God-created brain does that automatically for us. Every thing is by and through the power of God and must be consistent with His established laws.

The devil has taken advantage of God's laws, distorting and misusing them for his own ends. But just because evil exploits the laws of God doesn't cause God to change the rules.

There is a text that says, "Ask, and it shall be given you; seek, and ye shall find; knock, and it shall be opened unto you" (Luke 11:9). To ask, to look for, and to knock imply that as we pray we must be aware that God is the One who has put His will into motion by establishing the natural order of things. When we pray, we must recognize that what we are asking must be in harmony with the laws that God has already determined will govern our existence on this earth.

God will on special occasions do as He did for Joshua the day He made the sun stand still, or as He did for Hezekiah when He made the sun go backward. Though God can perform such miracles that seem to change natural law, we should not take this for granted. Our prayers should more often than not be in harmony with natural law. There is a danger that we pray that the car will run without fuel or that, if we stay up all night every night and eat nothing but Corn Curls, He will keep us healthy and strong. That is presumption.

In going to God in prayer, we must not only ask, but we must seek and knock. This means that we ourselves have a part to play in helping God to answer our prayers. For example, when a house catches on fire, we usually work to put out the fire before we try to figure out what caused it—but if my house is on fire and there is a broken gas main feeding that fire, knowledge of that fact is essential in effectively putting out the fire. To use an old illustration, if the bathtub is running over, the first thing to do is turn off the water and then start cleaning it up.

In our prayers we often ask God to solve some serious problem that in fact cannot be solved until its cause is located and dealt with.

One day I was asked to pray for a person who felt oppressed by the devil. I do not like to volunteer for this kind of thing, but when a person is seeking the help of God, I cannot refuse. I went with several of my colleagues to pray for the person. Before we prayed, as is my custom, I asked the person several questions. One of them was "Do you have bitterness and resentment against anyone?" The person, it turned out, was currently in therapy and did have tremendous bitterness and resentment against their parents. The therapist was apparently justifying these feelings.

I believe bitterness and resentment are the fertile soil in which the devil delights to gain access into a person's life. I felt that if we were going to pray for the devil to stop oppressing this person, we would need first to address the matter of the bitterness and resentment. We would need to ask God to forgive the spirit of bitterness and in its place give the person the gift of forgiveness.

I am sorry to report that although the person wanted to be free from the oppression of the devil, they felt that they had a perfect right to feel bitter and resentful toward their parents. They didn't want that problem brought into the prayer.

When we pray for the sick, the Bible teaches we ought to take seriously what might have led to the sickness. James 5:15 says that the prayer of faith will heal the sick, and if a person has committed any sins, they will be forgiven. Then it says in the next verse, "Confess your faults one to another, and pray for one another, that ye may be healed."

Although Jesus made it clear that a person is not necessarily afflicted because of what their mother or father did, He did make it clear that we ourselves might be responsible for many of our problems. When a person requests special prayer, we often pray for them, no questions asked. We should not pry into a person's life, but if our prayers for them are going to be successful, we must encourage the person to search their heart and life to ascertain if they have a part to play in solving their problem.

When we are sick, we would do well to try to find out where we have been out of harmony with the laws of God in the physical, emotional, and spiritual aspects of our lives.

Prayer is more than bending the knee, closing the eyes, and saying some special words or even invoking a supernatural power. It is the process by which we put ourselves firmly on the side of God and seek to cooperate with the principles that He has established. We should not ask Him to do something that is totally out of character with the way He has ordained things should be. To put it in plain language, our prayers should be in harmony with the laws of nature. Though He may sometimes choose to reveal His answer in ways that appear to change His natural laws, it is presumptuous for us to assume that He will make an exception except in the rarest of circumstances. And those circumstances will be decided by Him in His infinite wisdom, which in many cases we will have to wait to understand.

### Doing a Reality Check

1. What do the principles enunciated in this chapter have to do with your lifestyle?

2. Is there something in these principles that would have to do with the way we drive a car?

3. In our prayers are we asking God to make an exception to His natural laws?

### Fine-tuning Your Prayer Life

1. Make a short list of specific ways in which you covenant to cooperate with God in helping Him answer your prayers.

2. Choose two things on this list on which to concentrate. Notice how this affects your lifestyle, as well as your prayers.

### Prayer

Loving Father, we are so unstable. How thankful we are that You do not change the rules as You go. You change not. You are the same yesterday, today, and tomorrow. Forgive us for so often asking You to make an exception to Your rules for us. We realize if You did, this world would be in chaos.

Forgive us for not cooperating with Your laws. We know if You are going to answer our prayers, we must cooperate with You in every way we can.

May Your Spirit, who promises to bring things to our minds when we need them, help us remember always to do our part in our prayers. You are a wonderful God! We pray through Jesus Christ our Lord, amen.

# Chapter 13

# Barriers to Answered Prayer

omeone once asked me why we need to pray if God already knows everything. The question is legitimate, because Scripture tells us God knows even the secrets of our hearts (Ps. 44:21). We do not pray to inform God of what He already knows. The process of praying is one in which we are made aware of our own needs.

Sometimes we might think the Lord does not hear our prayers. Of course our omnipotent and omnipresent God hears and knows everything, even those prayers that don't seem to go any higher than the ceiling. It could be there are hindrances that keep Him from reaching us in answer to our prayers. But these are created by us, not by Him.

Sometimes our prayers, while within the will of God, are not answered because of other problems in our lives. If such a request were granted, it would be interpreted by us that God approves of or has chosen to overlook some serious character flaw that we might be ignoring.

I have been told that in the event of an emergency large jetliners can continue to fly on even one engine. Unfortunately, the Christian life will not fly on just one engine. Someone who ignores important character flaws, while at the same time expecting to grow spiritually will find their prayer life ineffective.

This chapter and the one that follows examine some of the serious barriers to answered prayer. These chapters could well be the most important in the entire book, with life-changing implications. The first barrier to answered prayer is selfishness.

### Selfish Prayers

"Ye ask, and receive not, because ye ask amiss, that ye may consume it upon your lusts" (James 4:3). Suppose we are praying for something we believe to be the will of God, but we are asking it for selfish reasons. This text tells us that to pray for selfish reasons is to pray "amiss." "The Lord seeth not as man seeth; for man looketh on the outward appearance, but the Lord looketh on the heart" (1 Sam. 16:7). Although what we are praying for may be the right thing and even for the glory of God, if we make the request for selfish reasons and the Lord were to answer our prayer, He would be encouraging our selfish attitude. We know that the principal purpose of prayer is to change the one who prays. Prayer answers affirming our pride and selfishness would frustrate the true purpose of prayer, which is to bring us into conformity to the will of God.

In my own life as a minister of the gospel, it could be entirely possible for my prayers that God would bless my ministry to be a conflict of interest with God! How could that be? Simply that my professional advancement has much to do with how I perceive the Lord's blessing my ministry. Can you see how I could be praying that the church be blessed and many souls won, but my prayer be prompted by the desire to make personal professional advancement and not for love of the kingdom?

A spouse could be praying for their unconverted partner not so much because they are really interested in their salvation, but because they are weary of harassment and ridicule. This is not to say we should never personally benefit or be blessed by answers to our prayers, but we need to ask ourselves as we pray why we are praying for a certain thing, and we need to beseech the Lord to purify our motives and deliver us from selfishness.

Another barrier to answered prayer is unconfessed sin.

### *Harboring Known Sin in the Life*

Two important texts must be considered here. One is Isaiah 59:2: "Your iniquities have separated between you and your God, and your sins have hid his face from you, that he will not hear." The other text is Psalm 66:18: "If I regard iniquity in my heart, the Lord will not hear me."

These passages are not suggesting that if we are sinners in the generic sense of the word, God will not hear our prayers. What is being referenced is known or cherished sin in the life. It is sin that we know to be wrong but that for some reason we rationalize away. Sometimes we will continue doing things that we know are wrong, assuring ourselves that nobody is perfect. We will even rationalize sin in our lives as a type of tradeoff. We know we are doing things that are definitely against the will of God, but we think our many good points somehow make up for all the negatives.

If we protect known sin in our lives, we will be inexorably attracted to error. Someone has rightly said that our theology is a reflection of our personal morality. This means that we are attracted to teachings that confirm our personal lifestyle. The significance of this is obvious. If we continue to harbor sin, we will be attracted to error and false doctrine as a bee is to honey.

Another danger of harboring known sin is the likelihood we will be led into fanaticism. The killdeer is a bird that nests on the ground. Should a person begin walking near where the killdeer is nesting, the parent will begin to feign injury. It may appear for all the world to have something wrong with its wing. Hopefully the person will be distracted by this ruse and begin to follow the parent, not knowing that they are being led farther away from the nest.

A person who is protecting a known sin will often begin to place great emphasis on a special virtue or point out a particular weakness in others. Consciously or unconsciously the effect is to draw attention away from the real problem in their own life. We must understand that cherished sin separates us from God and can result in all kinds of spiritual delusions and fantasies.

We often are aware that there is a particular sin in our life, but we try to play it down. A person might acknowledge a sin but feel it is only a small thing and doesn't have much importance. They may even claim to have given up all of the big sins in their lives and to have only a few insignificant ones left. I don't know if you have considered this or not, but the sins we hold on to are actually not the little ones but the big ones. We can know this because although we may have classified them as insignificant, they are the sins for which we are willing to trade our eternal life.

The story is told of a person who, sitting in the house of their heart one day, looked out the window and saw Jesus coming up the sidewalk. They looked around the living room. This was a surprise visit, and they really weren't ready for Jesus right then. So as He walked toward the door, they quickly threw some things they knew Jesus shouldn't see into the bedroom of their heart and closed the door to that room.

About that time they heard Jesus knocking and went to open the door and welcome Him in. They invited Him to sit down and began a friendly conversation. Pretty soon Jesus looked up and asked, "Where does that door lead?"

The host replied, "Lord, that is just the bedroom—You know, just a regular run-of-the-mill bedroom."

Jesus replied, "I would like to see it."

Knowing they had thrown things into the room they didn't want Jesus to see, the person said, "Just a minute, Lord." They went into the bedroom and threw the things into the closet. Then, smiling graciously, they invited Jesus to see the bedroom. He said little, but asked what that smaller door was and where it led. His host told Him it was just the closet.

Jesus said, "I would like to see that, too."

The point is obvious. When we invite Jesus into our heart, we must allow Him to clean up our heart in every detail so we both can feel comfortable about every aspect of our lives.

### Bitterness and Resentment

The most significant and perhaps the most common barrier to answered prayer is bitterness and resentment. "Forgive us our debts, as we forgive our debtors" (Matt. 6:12) is one of the most important statements in all the Bible having to do with the prayer life.

Forgiving those who have wronged us is not an option. Verses 14 and 15 tell us, "For if ye forgive men their trespasses, your heavenly Father will also forgive you: but if ye forgive not men their trespasses, neither will your Father forgive your trespasses."

The thought that immediately comes to mind is that this means we must forgive only those who have wronged us and who have said they were sorry. But forgiveness goes far beyond this. The Bible calls on us to forgive those who have wronged us and have not made it right. Notice the words "Forgive us our debts, as we forgive our debtors." Don't you see? They are still our debtors. They still owe us something. They have not asked for forgiveness or made things right with us.

We might insist, "But why does God insist that we forgive a person who is not sorry?" The answer is so that we can get on with our lives. I have talked with people who are bitter and resentful. One person had been wronged 40 years earlier. I could see in their face that it was as if it had happened just yesterday.

One day a particularly bitter and resentful young person said, "I don't know how I can ever forgive my mother for what she did to me." I asked how long ago it had been since she had been so aggrieved. "Twenty years" was the reply.

One day a person whose life had been badly damaged by another person came to my office. At one point in the conversation I asked if they had ever thought of praying for the other person.

"I surely do," they responded between gritted teeth. "I pray that they will get what they deserve!"

I remember the experience of another person whose daughter had been murdered by her husband. The daughter had married the boy next door. After a few years and one child, a little boy, the marriage went bad. Then one day, in a rage, the daughter's husband strangled her.

This former son-in-law had been tried and convicted and was serving a life sentence. The woman was given custody of her grandchild. The grandparent confessed to me that she was still so bitter that she found herself hating the grandson. The point is, bitterness and resentment soon spread to others in our lives.

Bitterness and resentment have a particular characteristic—they are omnipresent. Take a young man in Key West, Florida, who is bitter and resentful toward his father. The young man decides he is going to leave home. He tells the world he is fed up with his dad and wants to get him out of his life, and so he is going to go as far away from his dad as possible! He's going to Alaska.

Those older and wiser could inform this young man that even though he might leave Key West and go to Alaska, his dad is going along with him. His dad is going with him because he is in his mind! To the extent a person harbors bitterness against anyone, just so the memory of that person will always plague them. The person against whom we are bitter and resentful goes with us wherever we go. They are with us 24 hours a day, seven days a week. As long as we harbor bitterness, we can never get away from them.

A grandfather once came to my office and told me the story of his precious granddaughter who had been raped and murdered. The authorities had apprehended the killer, and he was in prison. This dear brother confessed that his life had become full of bitterness and resentment for what had happened. He found himself hating the murderer. But even worse, he began to discover his bitterness and resentment toward the murderer was beginning to spill over onto other people in his life until finally he discovered that it was now being directed toward God.

He recognized what was happening to him. The bitterness was like a cancer in his soul. So he fell to his knees one day and poured out his heart to God. He confessed his feelings and asked the Lord to forgive him and give him the gift of forgiveness.

What happened in this case? Be assured that the brother's prayer did not bring his granddaughter back to life. It didn't even convert the murderer. But it provided a wonderful miracle, nevertheless; it healed the heart of the grandfather, and now he could get on with his life.

When I was 18 years old, I worked on a plastering crew. One day we went out to stucco a house. We arrived early to make sure that the equipment and the materials were ready for us to work. We strung the extension cord for the electric cement mixer and plugged in the machine. The mixer switch was on when it had been unplugged, so the instant my friend plugged it in, the mixer paddles began to turn. There must have been something wrong with the tines on the plug, because as soon as my buddy dropped the cord on the ground, it disconnected. He picked it up and began to spread the tines so the connection would hold together. In the meantime I noticed there were some twigs in the bottom of the mixer. The very instant I put my arm into the mixer to get the twigs out, my friend plugged in the cord. Instantly the motor started up and the mixer paddles caught and broke my arm. Of course, I screamed in pain. My buddy didn't ask what was wrong; he immediately unplugged the cord. It was not a moment too soon. In another second the machine would have taken my arm off at the shoulder. We got into the truck and sped to the hospital emergency room. At first the pain was dull, then sharp and fierce. After what seemed hours, my arm was set in a cast.

When a specialist came to see me, he said that because of the nature of the fracture it would not heal cleanly but would leave a knot of bone at the site of the break. This knot would make it impossible for me to rotate my forearm. He suggested doing what is called an open reduction. This would require a surgical procedure to insert a stainless steel pin down the center of each bone in my lower arm through and past the point of the fracture. This would align them properly and avoid the knot. He said the surgery would leave some large scars, but at least I would be able to move my arm freely.

I told him to go ahead, and he did. To this day I have two large scars and two smaller ones on my right forearm. They are there for life. I am telling you this story to illustrate that though the scars are permanent, the pain is gone!

You may have been badly hurt by someone or something in your past, but you cannot live your life over again. The damage is done. Life is not like the story of a teenager who, after his first automobile accident, prayed, "Lord, help that accident not to have happened!" We are wasting our time if we pray like that. Though we will carry for life the scars of what has happened to us, we can, however, ask the Lord to take away the pain. He does this by giving us the gift of forgiveness. But make no mistake, if we continue to hold bitterness and resentment in our hearts, it becomes a hindrance to our prayers. Remember the mother whose daughter had been strangled? I asked her if she had prayed that God would give her the gift of forgiveness. She confessed she had almost given up praying, adding that she thought if she asked the Lord to give her a spirit of forgiveness it would mean she didn't care anymore that her daughter had been killed.

I explained that a wrong committed will always be a wrong. When Jesus prayed, "Father, forgive them; for they know not what they do" (Luke 23:34), He didn't mean what they were doing was right. Do you see? That prayer simply enables us to get on with our lives and experience a new start. Bitterness and resentment stop our lives. Forgiveness gives us a new start!

### Doing a Reality Check

1. Certainly you and I are praying for others—for family and friends. Ask yourself why you are praying for them. Is it for their benefit or for your own?

2. We are all sinners. Yet in Christ we must be repentant sinners. Has there been a pet sin in your life you know shouldn't be there? What is it?

3. Examine your heart to see if there is anyone against whom you are holding bitterness and resentment.

### Fine-tuning Your Prayer Life

1. When you pray for a loved one, try to see them as God sees

them. Is there anything you are doing that could be hindering God's work in their life? Ask Jesus to forgive you.

2. Read Romans 6:17. Every time you see the word "sin," substitute the name of a specific sin with which you struggle. Ask Jesus to forgive you and give you victory.

3. Forgiveness is a gift. Ask Jesus to forgive you for your bitterness toward (name the person), and ask Him to give you the gift of forgiveness. You will need to pray this prayer many times. Don't be like the woman who prayed that the person would "get what they deserved." Pray for your enemies as you would pray for the people most important in your life. I have done that, and the Lord has healed me!

### *Prayer*

God, this chapter has been almost too heavy for us to bear. Thank You for bringing us under conviction of some really serious areas of our lives. When we see the way we really are, we understand why the apostle Paul cried out, "O wretched man that I am! who shall deliver me from the body of this death?" [Rom. 7:24]. But You have promised to deliver us. You are the one who forgives and doesn't hold our past against us.

As You gave sight to the blind, and made the deaf to hear, and even raised dead people, heal us of the things that are a disgrace to You and that are ruining the quality of our lives. Especially heal us of our bitterness and resentment. Give us, O God, the wonderful gift of forgiveness. We know You can, You will, and You already have. Amen.

# Chapter 14

# More Barriers
# to Answered Prayer

There is an old saying that we should put first things first. Nowhere is this more true than in the matter of prayer. Imagine how you would feel if a person who claimed to be your friend borrowed a large sum of money but never made any attempt to pay it back. Not only that, but this person who claimed to be your friend treated all your other friends very badly. To make matters infinitely more complicated, this so-called friend was actually responsible for the death of your only child. At times they seemed to have remorse, but at other times it seemed as though they didn't really care.

To add insult to injury, this person would not talk with you except to ask for something they couldn't get anywhere else. Then they would flatter you and tell you how much they appreciated you, completely ignoring all the wrong they had done to you.

Do you see a parallel here? God is most eager to hear from us. He welcomes our prayers. Yet if our relationship with Him is going to mean anything more than an attempt to exploit Him for what we can get, we are going to need to take some things into account before we pray. God is willing to give good gifts to His children (Matt. 7:11), yet what He wants most is that we be healed of sin and all the dysfunction that it represents.

How could an earthly father focus on preparing for his child's college education while the child was afflicted with a life-threatening disease? Naturally the cure of the child would take priority. Just so, our loving heavenly Father, who has many gifts for us, has as His first concern that we be healed from the malady of sin that has so badly affected our quality of life. This is why He wants us to pray to *be*—and His priority must be ours!

Perhaps you have seen the poster that says, "If you feel far from God, guess who moved?" God's relationship to us never changes, but our relationship to Him is often very unstable, to say the least. This is why it is important that when we pray, we need first to make sure we are tuned to His frequency.

Before we come to God in prayer, we must take the opportunity to review our lives and ask His forgiveness for getting off track. We need to ask that His Spirit will be able to speak to our hearts without any obstacles blocking the way. The promise is that if we confess our sins, He is faithful and just to forgive us our sins. The best part, perhaps the most important part, is that He has promised to cleanse us from all unrighteousness (1 John 1:9).

### Putting Others Before God

Another obstacle to prayer is created when we put others before God. "Son of man, these men have set up their idols in their heart, and put the stumblingblock of their iniquity before their face: should I be enquired of at all by them?" (Eze. 14:3).

An idol is not just an image made of wood or stone or precious metals. An idol, as far as God is concerned, is whatever we esteem above Him. A person may say, "Not a problem; I have given God first place in my life." But what does it mean to give God first place in our lives?

Suppose one day I take my wife, Betty, out to eat at her favorite restaurant. I buy flowers for the occasion. Then, by candlelight, and at just the right moment, I look into her eyes and say, "Betty, I love you very much. You have first place in my life. But you should know about Judy, Sarah, and Patty. They have second, third, and fourth places in my life!"

"Ridiculous!" you say. Of course you are right. My wife has not only first place in my life as far as women are concerned, but all the other places as well. She preempts the relationship I might have with other women I meet.

When we say we have given God first place in our lives, it means there is no place in our lives where He is not. In other words, we do not put God on the top shelf and then the rest of our lives on the other shelves. When God is on the top shelf, He must be on every other shelf, also!

Many consider that their lives have two aspects—a religious side and a secular side. This thinking creates many problems. The truth is, our lives are either all sacred or they are all profane. We must be able to bring God into our everyday, workaday life, not just our Sabbath life. We must pray for our commitment to our heavenly Father to permeate every phase of our existence.

No man can love his wife and children too much. But he can put them before God. Honestly ask yourself if God has absolutely first place in your life.

### Problems Between Husbands and Wives

The next barrier to answered prayer is literally close to home! "Ye husbands, dwell with them according to knowledge, giving honour unto the wife, as unto the weaker vessel, and as being heirs together of the grace of life; that your prayers be not hindered" (1 Peter 3:7). Although this text is directed to men, there is no doubt it is talking to wives also, and for that matter, to the way we all treat each other, whether we be married or single.

There are men who pretend to be Christians who are often unkind, if not brutal, to their wives. There are wives who are faithful and devoted to the church, yet are habitually cross and wound their husbands by the sharpness of their speech and their unruly tempers. Then there is the matter of how parents often treat their children and how children often relate to their parents. Often the most difficult place to be a Christian is in the home. I have come to the conclusion that if your Christianity doesn't work at home, it won't work anywhere. I am sorry to say that sometimes we treat total strangers with more kindness and courtesy than we treat those with whom we live.

We are admonished that our homes are to be little heavens on earth. Unfortunately, for many that isn't the case. Someone was overheard to say they couldn't wait to leave the office and go home, where they didn't have to be kind anymore! Can you imagine how our homes would be if we treated those we love as politely and with the same courtesy we might give to customers? If we would practice kindness everywhere, our homes would indeed be little bits of heaven. I have personally found that when my relationship with Betty is strained, it strains my relationship with God (1 John 4:20). When my relationship with God is strained, it strains my relationship with my wife. By God's grace I make it a priority every day to keep things right with God as well as with Betty! The point, in view of 1 Peter 3:7, is that we cannot separate our relationship with God from how we treat our spouses.

### Insincere Prayer

Another barrier to answered prayer is insincerity. Psalm 145:18 says, "The Lord is nigh unto all them that call upon him, to all that call upon him in truth." It may sound incongruous, but it is possible that many of our prayers are not sincere. By that I mean they do not represent what we really want, but rather what we feel obligated to say.

How many times do we pray to the Lord because we are afraid of consequences? Fear as a prayer motivator is badly flawed. Could it be that many requests we make are because we are afraid of what might happen to us if we don't involve the Lord? A person could pray for the Lord to give them victory over a bad temper, not because of a conviction that a bad temper is un-Christlike, but because their spouse is threatening to leave them if they don't do something about it. What is wrong with that? Simply that someone persuaded against their will is of the same opinion still. The person who sincerely comes to recognize that their bad temper is a sin against God and asks Him to give them the victory will receive it. On the other hand, a person who is simply trying to appease a spouse may fall back to their old ways when the situation seems to indicate it is safe to do so.

Another prayer driver is often guilt. God uses guilt to tell us when we are off the track. Guilt can function like the gauges in my car that tell me the engine is overheating. I respond to the warning because I am committed to maintaining my car in the best condition possible. That guilt motivates me to correct the problem.

Guilt plays an important and necessary role in the life of a person who is committed to Jesus. Such a person learns to appreciate the fact that the Holy Spirit has been given to convict us of sin.

But consider the person who has not made a heart commitment to Jesus as their Lord and Saviour. They resent feeling guilty and try to suppress their feelings as they pray. They really don't feel what they are doing is wrong, but inasmuch as the Lord seems to be sensitive about some of the things they like to do, they pray to keep on His good side.

Duty may be another negative prayer motivator for some. They may respond when the preacher presents a sermon on the need to pray. Or their spouse or a friend may tell them they ought to pray about this or that. So to humor the minister or their friends, they will go through the motions. But this kind of prayer is not very fulfilling. Those who have conducted smoking-cessation programs say that often people come to the program because a spouse has told them they ought to stop smoking. The success rate is not very high until they themselves want to quit.

The implications are obvious. If our prayers are being driven by fear, guilt, or duty, they will soon become burdensome and will most likely fall away over time.

When we pray truthfully, from the depths of our hearts, the results will be completely different. Not only will we experience great victories and growth in our lives, but we will actually enjoy the experience!

An anonymous author has written, " 'Tis not enough to bend the knee and words of prayer to say. The heart must with the lips agree, or else we do not pray."

Look into your heart and ask if there is some obvious obstacle in your life that might be hindering your prayers. I say obvious for a reason. Many times we ignore or try to suppress the obvious problems in our lives. Instead we try to locate a problem we may have forgotten or identify one that hasn't happened yet. We need to live our lives in the present. Let us pray that God will give us strength to overcome the obvious, and that we will then be set free to continue to grow in grace and in the knowledge of our Lord and Saviour Jesus Christ.

### Doing a Reality Check

1. What is the most important thing in our lives right now?

2. Do you treat total strangers more charitably than you treat members of the family?

3. What do you really want God to do for you?

### Fine-tuning Your Prayer Life

1. If you are aware that you have said unkind words to a member of the family, ask them to forgive you.

2. Make definite plans as to how you will put God into every aspect of your life. How different will things be from the way they are now?

### Prayer

Holy Father, the more we think about it, the more we are aware that without Your mercy and grace we cannot survive. Unless You forgive us and cleanse us every day, we will not be able to go on. We have given our lives to You, and You have told us no one can take us out of Your hand.

Lord, in so many places our families are falling apart. We have become so preoccupied with the things of this world, and the devil is ruining us. Father, as You delivered David from the giant, please deliver us from the giant problems in our lives. We confess we are responsible for many of them. Please finish what You have begun in our hearts, as You promised. Amen and amen.

# Chapter 15

# The Devil Also Answers Prayer

omewhere around 1988 I began to get serious about prayer. Of course, I had been praying before that time, but I was passing through some real crises. Have you noticed that something happens to us when we experience trouble in our lives? We do not continue the way we were. We either get closer to God or we drift away from Him.

When we suppose we have control of our lives, we tend to give prayer a low priority. But when "the angry billows roll o'er my tempest-driven soul," we suddenly begin to pray as never before. That is what happened to me.

I also began looking for books on prayer. The Adventist Book Centers yielded little more than *The ABC's of Prayer*, by dear brother Glenn Coon. He was a pioneer in the science of prayer in our denomination. Other Christian bookstores had a few more, but not a lot. Someone told me about a series of books by E. M. Bounds, a preacher who lived in the 1800s. Other prayer classics were *With Christ in the School of Prayer*, by Andrew Murray, and *The Kneeling Christian*, by an anonymous author. I bought whatever I could find, as well as biographies of great men and women of prayer.

There may have been a famine of books on prayer 10 years ago, but that is not the situation now. Prayer is in. It could be said that anybody who is anybody these days is into prayer. Football teams pray before games, and it is not uncommon to see a basketball player run onto the floor making the sign of the cross. A friend of mine saw a video of the singer Madonna kneeling down to pray before going out for one of her concerts. A heavyweight boxer gave Jesus the credit for helping him knock out his opponent. When prayer becomes this popular, we should begin to be on our guard. It would not be unthinkable for the devil to take advantage of all the interest in prayer and work to subvert and corrupt it

Not only are a lot of people talking to God these days, but a lot of people are saying that God talks to them. They say "God told me this" or "God told me that." Seemingly prayer is now everyone's direct line to heaven. But there can be a danger in this view of prayer. Someone once told me, "I don't care what the Bible says; I know what God told me!" Many are claiming a special revelation from God to put a holy stamp on their own opinions. At a time when the sufficiency of Scripture is under attack, we must beware of thinking that we are somehow receiving revelations from God that are on a par with Scripture.

Does God give us impressions? He most certainly does. But His impressions are always in harmony with all of Scripture, and not with just an isolated verse here or there.

There may have been a time when we were not praying enough. Could it be said that we are now praying too much? Is that possible? Could it be that prayer is being trivialized or, worse still, that the devil is trying to infiltrate our prayer life?

I clipped an article out of a newspaper not long ago. It carried the heading "1 Million Brazilians Pray Rio Will Be Host of Games." An estimated 1 million Brazilians had stood on Rio's famous Copacabana Beach one Sunday and offered a "prayer to heaven" that their country would be selected as host of the 2004 Olympic Games. The mass prayer was Rio's final effort to persuade the International Olympic Committee to choose the city as the Olympic site.

Each year approximately a quarter million people gather in Daytona Beach, Florida, for Bikers' Week. A newspaper report of the event included a picture of a priest blessing a Harley-Davidson motorcycle with holy water. It said the bikes were blessed after a special bikers' mass and barbecue on Sunday morning. These events and others like them show how prayer has become popularized in today's society. In the past whenever a spiritual value became popular, it quickly became corrupted.

Prayer has been described as "the opening of the heart to God as to a friend" *(Steps to Christ,* p. 93). Jesus says to us, "Behold, I stand at the door, and knock" (Rev. 3:20). But there are many other interests that knock at the door of our heart. Before we open the door, we must be careful to ascertain who is knocking.

One evening a few months ago there was a knock at the front door of our home. As I went to the door I looked first through the frosted glass. Standing outside was a woman I did not recognize.

When I opened the door, she said, "Hello! I am your neighbor from down the street." When she said that, I wanted to respond, "I thought I had met all our neighbors, but I have never seen you." When I asked which house she lived in, she said it was the second one down the street. What could I say? So I invited her in. I asked her name, which she said was Carol. "What can I do for you, Carol?" I asked.

She explained that unexpected company had just arrived at her house and that she needed to borrow some beer for them. When she asked if we had any, a little shiver went down my back. I said, "I won't be able to help you, because we don't drink beer." Then sensing that something was not right, I stepped toward her and said, "Carol, I don't know what you're up to, but I think you should leave."

She didn't object, but walked out and turned in the direction she claimed to live. I waited a minute and then went out to the sidewalk. I saw her turn in to the second house, but then in a moment she came back down the walk and went to the third house. I caught up with her and asked, "Carol, who are you, and what are you doing here? Is there someone waiting for you out at the main road? You'd better leave now, or I'll have to call the police."

Mumbling something about getting lost, she walked down to the main road and disappeared from view. Obviously she was giving a made-up story in order to get alcohol. The neighbors across the street came out and said she had approached them earlier in the day, and they had given her a bottle of wine. I don't know what eventually happened to Carol.

The point is that when she said she was my neighbor, my defenses went down and I felt obligated to open my home to her. I did learn a lesson. It is not safe to throw open the door and let just anybody in.

Prayer is the opening of the heart. Prayer can be dangerous if we open our hearts without being aware of who may come in. Just as we must know who is knocking on the door of our houses, so we must know to whom we are opening our hearts in prayer. But how can we know? Friend, the Bible is like a security peephole that lets us know who is trying to get into our hearts when we pray. If we pray outside the context of the revealed Word of God, we should be suspicious about any answers we might receive.

There is an enormous amount of answered prayer being reported these days. If all the prayers that people say are being answered are being answered from God, then our God is not a God of order but of anarchy! Is God really helping boxers knock each other out?

Could it be that Satan is answering a lot of prayers these days? And why not? If, like a computer virus, he can infiltrate our prayers, he will be able to hollow out our spiritual lives. The result will be, as the Bible predicted, a generation with "a form of godliness, but denying the power thereof" (2 Tim. 3:5).

Can't you imagine what the devil is saying to his imps? "Listen, boys, get them praying about everything, but keep them selfish and outside the Word of God. As they begin praying for anything and everything, answer their prayers like crazy. They will think God is doing it to show He accepts them just as they are, so they will have no incentive to let Him change them. Then we will have them."

Matthew 7:22, 23 suggests the devil does answer prayers: "Many will say to me in that day, Lord, Lord, have we not prophesied in thy name? and in thy name have cast out devils? and in thy name done many wonderful works? And then will I profess unto them, I never knew you: depart from me, ye that work iniquity."

This group had been praying that the Lord would do all kinds of miracles, and apparent miracles had come in answer to their prayers. Yet the Lord denied having had anything to do with it.

One Sunday my father-in-law saw a TV minister preaching about the Ten Commandments. The minister told his congregation and his viewers that Christians should obey the commandments. When the program was over, my father-in-law sat down and wrote the pastor a letter thanking him for the sermon and asking, inasmuch as he advocated keeping the commandments, why he didn't keep the Sabbath of the fourth commandment.

The pastor was kind enough to reply. The first part of the letter gave the usual list of reasons people give for keeping Sunday, using the few out-of-context first-day texts from the New Testament. The last paragraph of the letter was the clincher. It said, "If God wanted me to keep the Sabbath, He wouldn't be blessing me the way that He is."

A Sundaykeeper once told me that the Lord had healed her back problem. She said that if He wanted her to keep the Sabbath, He wouldn't have healed her. For her, the healing was proof that she was keeping the right day.

Long ago I came to the conclusion that we are running a risk when we use a material yardstick to measure the blessings of God. This is obvious in the cases just mentioned. There is no doubt that the Lord does bless us with material blessings. Yet at the same time, if material prosperity is always an indication of God's approval, we would be compelled to conclude that even the Mafia must be doing something right!

Our prayers will be largely ineffective and in many cases outright dangerous unless we sit down with God's Word and discover His will in the particular thing we are praying about.

There is yet another side. Some people already know what the will of God is, but pray for just the opposite. Little wonder that our prayers in many cases are bouncing off the ceiling, not because we do not know what the will of God is, but because we are refusing to do it or are expecting a special dispensation.

One young woman, about to marry a non-Christian, assured me that she had prayed about it and felt sure that it was what God wanted her to do. Forget the admonition about not being joined together with unbelievers (2 Cor. 6:14). That never entered into the decision. To ascertain God's will correctly, we must put our own feelings aside and obey the plainly spoken "Thus saith the Lord."

When we are praying outside of the will of God, we are subjecting ourselves to the possibility that Satan will answer our prayers. When this happens, we will become hopelessly deceived, because we will see the answer to prayer as a sign of God's approval of the way we are living or what we happen to be doing at the time. To pray outside of the will of God is dangerous. This generation has become increasingly more self-centered and materialistic. Instead of using prayer to commit to do the will of God, many are using prayer to manipulate and control circumstances for their own purposes. Prayer can be downright dangerous! Prayer outside the Word of God can be a tool of the enemy. Let me put it plainly now. The devil answers prayer. Our only safety is to make sure that our prayers are firmly rooted and grounded in the Word of God.

### Doing a Reality Check

1. What yardstick do you use to determine if God is answering your prayers?

2. Do you think we ought to ask God for anything our heart desires? What could be the result of doing this?

3. How might we be using prayer to manipulate others?

4. How can we be sure it is God who is impressing our hearts? (Look up Isaiah 8:20.)

### Fine-tuning Your Prayer Life

1. Compile a list of blessings you believe the Lord has given you. Do not include anything material or physical. Remember, the priority of prayer is not to get, but to *be*.

2. Think of ways in which your prayer life might become trivial-

ized. List the top five things you have been praying that God will do for you. In view of what you have been learning about the priority of prayer, put the requests in their order of importance from God's perspective. Are there any that might be left out or put farther down on the list?

### Prayer

Dear God, we tend to think like the world does. We tend to count Your blessings in dollars and cents. Now we realize our material prosperity may be a concession from the dark side unless we have committed ourselves to seek first the kingdom of heaven and Your righteousness.

Teach us to measure Your blessings by the fruit of the Spirit in our lives, because we know this can come only from You. In Jesus' name, amen.

# Chapter 16

# The When and Where of Effective Prayer

Time is significant in the Christian life. Although we do not all have the same amount of wealth or talents and abilities, we all have time. While we may not all have the same amount of quantitative time—some of us may live longer than others—yet at this moment we all have time.

To talk about giving our lives to Jesus, to talk about living the Christian life and all that goes with it, is ultimately to talk about time. We do not all have the ability to give God the same quantity of money, just as we do not have the ability to dedicate the same talents to Him. But we do all have the same amount of time at any particular moment.

We can choose to dedicate what time we have either to God or to ourselves. Jesus once told a story about a man who went out to plant a field (Luke 8:5-15). In those days they didn't drill the wheat into the ground with machinery; they simply threw it out by hand. Those with experience could accomplish this in a fairly even manner. But no matter how proficient a person became at broadcasting the seed evenly in the prepared areas, some of it would land in out-of-the-way places. Jesus said some of the seed fell on the roadway, where the birds ate it. Other seed fell on the stones by the edge of the field and dried up because there was no soil for the roots. More seed fell among thorns, which overshadowed the growing plants and choked them out.

Jesus told His listeners that the seed in the story represents the

Word of God. The various environments where the seed fell represent the different attitudes in our lives.

Some of the seed fell among the thorns. Jesus later explained to His disciples that by thorns He meant the cares of this life that choke out the spiritual growth.

A popular grass often used on Florida lawns is called St. Augustine. It is very thick and grows by sending runners across the top of the ground. A person can plant plugs of this grass, which will soon spread until it covers the whole area. When we first moved to Florida, our front lawn was a common native grass called Bahia. Bahia is thin and not particularly pretty. My neighbor had the St. Augustine variety, and amazingly, in a few years my neighbor's nice St. Augustine grass simply spread across my front lawn and choked out the Bahia. (Well, naturally, I also put in some plugs to encourage things along.)

Now my lawn is composed of the coveted St. Augustine grass. I have to be careful now, because there are other grasses continually trying to choke out the St. Augustine. One of these is a persistent variety called India crabgrass. If it is allowed a small start, it climbs across the top of the St. Augustine. As it gets thicker and thicker, the sun isn't able to reach the St. Augustine, and it dies out. Many people's spiritual life isn't going anywhere because it is simply being choked out by the cares of this life—the other things that they are spending their time on.

Life is about time. If we are going to have a thriving spiritual life, we have to spend time at it. If we are going to have a good golf score, it requires practice, and practice is about time. If we are going to make progress in any area of our lives, we are going to have to spend time at it. Our lives are a reflection of how we spend our time. It may sound too simple, but the person who has a growing Christian life is the person who is spending time at it.

The cares of this life are all but choking out the spiritual lives of countless people. These days both parents are usually working. We start the day early and go to bed late. Many of us have a high standard of living as far as material things go, but a very poor standard of living in the things that really matter.

Many complain that modern life leaves them no time for spiritual things. The truth is we have the same amount of time we ever did. The question is How have we chosen to spend it? To be able to pray effectively, we must allocate time. Time is the raw material of life. If we want a spiritual life that means anything, if we are going to experience what it means to be a victorious and growing Christian, we are going to have to set aside time to make it happen.

When it comes to prayer, some people think we can pray while doing everything else. Although it is true we can do other things and be praying at the same time, we can't be thinking about other things and be praying at the same time. If prayer is going to be a priority in our lives, we must set aside time to pray—time when we are not doing anything else.

People who are growing spiritually, who enjoy what it means to be overcomers, and who know the meaning and life-changing power of prayer are the people who have set aside a special time every day to be alone with God. These people have learned that the Christian life goes best when they begin the day with God. If we want to pray effectively, we must set apart time for it.

There is a difference between making time for prayer and setting aside time for prayer. We cannot make time for prayer, because time is fixed. There are only 24 hours in a day. If until now you have not been spending time with the Lord, there will be no time to fit it in. I say this because your time is now occupied with other things. Whenever we decide that we are going to put something new into our lives, we are going to have to take something out to make room for it.

At the beginning of the year people make New Year's resolutions. Studies show that these new resolutions last only five days on the average. This is because the new resolutions are placed on top of everything else.

One day my wife asked me to go out and get our son's work clothes, which he had left in the car. It was raining hard, as it usually does on a summer afternoon in Florida, where we live. I took the clothes basket in one hand and an umbrella in the other and went out to the car to get the clothes. I had to balance the umbrella while I put the clothes in the basket. That day there were more dirty work clothes than there was room in the basket, so rather than make a second trip, I heaped the clothes up, actually overfilling the basket. I held the load close to my body and returned to the house. But as I walked, the clothes began falling out onto the ground.

The clothes that fell out were not the ones in the basket, but those that were heaped on top. The point is that when we decide to pray, we often add prayer to all the things that are already occupying our time. The result is that the prayer soon falls out. We will not be able to add prayer time to our lives until we make room for it, and that will mean taking out something else that is less important. We don't make time for prayer; we set aside time for prayer.

### A Place for Prayer

To experience the true joy of communion with God, we also need to have a special place for prayer. This is logical, because when a person is trying to spend quality time with someone, they should be alone with them. Of course, we can pray to God in any place and at any time. But the most effective and meaningful time is spent alone with God in a special place.

It is no secret that marriages thrive when the husband and wife have special quality time together at special places. It is the same in our relationship with Jesus.

Jesus used to have special places for prayer. Others must have known where those places were, because Judas knew where Jesus would be praying when he led the crowd to arrest Him.

The Bible tells us that we should have a special place for prayer. Matthew 6:6 says, "When thou prayest, enter into thy closet, and when thou hast shut thy door, pray to thy Father which is in secret; and thy Father which seeth in secret shall reward thee openly." Of course, Jesus is not talking about a literal closet; He is talking about a special place to be alone without distractions.

To be alone with God is not easy. Prayer and time spent alone with

God in a special place is a discipline. We have to work at it to make it happen. We need to be careful, though, because a person can actually be alone with someone physically and not really be there at all.

We can be thinking of other things while communing with God. So getting alone with God in a special place doesn't mean it is going to be easy from there on. We must learn to concentrate. We must know what we are doing there and why.

We are so used to being distracted that many of us do not know how to be alone or even feel uncomfortable when we are alone. This is because we are used to having the radio playing, the TV on, or the kids interrupting. We are not accustomed to being in the silence of our own contemplation.

But when we are alone with God, we must learn how to be silent and to endure and enjoy silence. The Scripture tells us, "Be still, and know that I am God" (Ps. 46:10). It is not in noise and hoopla that we get to know God best, but in the stillness. As we make plans to move forward in our prayer life, we will want to have a special place where we go for our quiet time with God.

### Understanding the Presence of God

We do not begin a conversation with someone until we are in their presence. A heart-to-heart talk is impossible unless the person we are talking to is present. When we talk about being alone with God, we think of being in His presence. What does it mean to be in the presence of God?

God cannot be seen with our eyes, nor under regular circumstances do we hear His voice with our ears. We cannot touch Him with our hands. In other words, our physical senses do not reveal God to us. How then do we go about being in the presence of Someone we do not see or who, at least as far as our five senses are concerned, is not there with us?

These physical limitations do not mean that we can't enjoy the presence of God. It is possible to enjoy someone's presence when they are not with us physically. We often do this by telephone. We also feel a special presence when we receive a letter from someone we love. Before we married, Betty lived in Florida and I lived in Ohio. We tried to write to each other nearly every day. When I came home from work, the first thing I asked my mother was "Is there a letter from Betty?" I was able to enjoy her presence though the letters she wrote me.

When we lived in South America, an American on work assignment there for several months came to my house because he had heard I had a shortwave radio. He had promised his wife that on their twentieth wedding anniversary they would publicly renew their vows. The twentieth anniversary was coming up, and here he was in South America. So he asked me if I would officiate at a ceremony to renew his vows over the shortwave radio. He had made arrangements to have her listening at a certain frequency at a certain time. And so when the day arrived, there we were in Santiago, Chile, and she was in the United States. They renewed their vows by shortwave radio, although they were thousands of miles apart.

On another occasion I was in Puerto Rico holding meetings when I received a phone call that a dear friend of mine had been diagnosed with bone cancer. They wanted to anoint him immediately, so you can guess what happened: I participated in the anointing by telephone. It was a special experience I will remember for a long time.

In the final analysis, isn't experiencing someone's presence essentially an inner experience? When we are in a friend's presence, isn't the realization and the enjoyment and even the significance of their presence something that goes beyond their physical presence and takes place within the heart? A friend may be on the other side of the room, but the real experience of their presence is within our own consciousness.

Jesus told the woman at the well, "God is a Spirit: and they that worship him must worship him in spirit and in truth" (John 4:24). On another occasion Jesus said, "I will love him and will manifest myself to him. . . . My Father will love him, and we will come unto him, and make our abode with him" (John 14:21-23). And so in a way we cannot yet fully understand but can surely appreciate, we may experience the presence of God deep down in our own consciousness—even though our five senses don't perceive Him. As Scripture says: "Whom having not seen, ye love" (1 Peter 1:8). It is through prayer that this mysterious but real experience is made possible.

At one time or another we may have thought that if Jesus were only here physically, the devotional life would be easier. But would it be? He was here physically at one time, yet the people who knew Him either loved Him or hated Him. To some He was just an ordinary person; to others He was a disappointment. But to others He was the Son of God, and this is the way it is today. Jesus told Thomas that those who would believe on Him without seeing Him would have an even greater blessing than those who had seen Him in person.

The Bible teaches that God is present everywhere. That means wherever we may be, God knows all about us. That means that He is accessible, and that no matter where we are, He can hear us; and that He loves us and helps us (Ps. 139:8). He is as near to us in one place as in any other. If we seek Him with all our hearts, the Scripture tells us we will find Him (Deut. 4:29).

Though distance cannot separate us from God, one thing that will separate us is sin. Sin doesn't make it impossible for God to see us, but rather it makes it impossible for us to discern His presence. For this reason the most important factor in being in the presence of God is that we must be in an attitude of repentance, with our sins confessed, and with the knowledge that, having confessed our sins, "He is faithful and just to forgive us our sins, and to cleanse us from all unrighteousness" (1 John 1:9).

### Communication Is a Two-way Street

Prayer is our part in communicating with God, but communication must be a two-way street. We must not only communicate with God; we must let Him communicate with us.

God has communicated with the human race through various methods. In the beginning it was face-to-face. Since sin He has communicated with us through His prophets. All along the way He communicates His majesty and power through His created works (Ps. 19:1). And His most wonderful communication to us was sending His Son to live among us (1 John 1:1). God has continued to communicate with us through the voice of the Holy Spirit, which impresses our hearts. In this day and age the basis for all God's communication with us is the Bible. It is the fountain from which His voice speaks to us. The Holy Spirit will impress our hearts, but it will always impress us consistent with the Word. This is very important to keep in mind.

Many millions of clocks and watches in the world are measuring time, but time is measured and calculated by the movement of the stars. You and I may have a clock or a watch that tells the time, but actually it may not be the accurate time at all. Although clocks are made to tell time, they do not control the essence of time. The God of the stars is in charge of that. It is God, then, not my watch, who is in control of the passage of time.

As the stars are the only reliable communicators of time, so the Word of God is the only reliable communicator of the voice of God to us. Although God may communicate with us in our heart or through our conscience, this communication should not be considered reliable unless it is tested by the Bible. Just as our watches may stop or gain time or lose time and so not give the correct time at all, we must not depend on an inner voice to guide us as to what is right and what is wrong. While it is true that the Holy Spirit communicates with our hearts, the Bible clearly tells us we cannot trust our own hearts. It tells us there is a way that seems right to us, but it is wrong (Prov. 16:25). God's thoughts and ours are not on the same wavelength (Isa. 55:8).

In our communion with God, the Bible must be the yardstick by which we measure the thoughts and ideas that we perceive are from Him. The foundation of God's communication with us will always be His Word. And in the same way, the base of our communication with Him must rest on the same foundation.

### *Giving God the Time of Day*

Our heavenly Father wishes we would give Him back some of the time He has given us. The practical fact is that if we spend only a little time with Him, He can give us only a little help. But if we will spend much time with Him, He will give us much help.

We are creatures of habit. We prefer doing things without thinking very hard. We often decide what we are going to do in a particular instance and then put ourselves on autopilot. But when it comes to faith and morals, our instincts are usually wrong. We may have a good sense of direction or of business, we may have many other natural abilities, but a person doesn't have a natural instinct to do what is right. Someone said that when we get into a moral problem, if we will decide what to do and then do the opposite, we will probably come closer to doing the right thing!

You have heard it said we ought to think before we speak. What would happen if we would pray before we spoke? Imagine what would happen if we were to say a little prayer before we made a phone call, or if we were to say a little prayer when someone was about to come into the office to talk to us! What would happen if we were to say a little prayer when the kids were about to come home from school, or our spouse was about to come home from work?

Part of my responsibilities has been overseeing the health screening vans in the Florida Conference. One day the man overseeing the mechanical details of the vans called to tell me of the condition of one of the vans that had just been returned from a church. Apparently someone had used duct tape to attach signs to the outside of the vehicle. Duct tape is very sticky and sometimes leaves adhesive when it is removed from a surface.

I felt myself becoming upset. It occurred to me that the people who had affixed the duct tape to the conference van wouldn't have thought of putting duct tape on one of their own cars. I decided that I would call up the church pastor and tell him off! But then it occurred to me that it would not be the Christlike thing to do. But I was still upset. So I decided that I would call him up and tell him off in a Christlike way!

Before I dialed, I thought that maybe I would say a little prayer. I prayed, and you can guess what I did next. I hung up the phone.

The reality is that we are often not sensitive to the way we treat others, and our reaction to how others treat us causes untold and unnecessary grief. The average person doesn't realize they are doing something wrong until it has already happened. What if we could be aware before we said or did something that we were about to make a mistake. We could then cry out to the Lord, and He would hear us. He is waiting and eager for that type of prayer.

Most of the suffering in our day-to-day lives is because we do not pray as we should. We have learned not to stick our finger in the blades of a fan or on a hot iron, but we don't seem to understand that the way we talk to our spouses could very well be destroying our marriages little by little. If we are not spending quality time every day alone with God, the problems and complexities of life are going to overwhelm us.

Some people think that somehow they can stay ahead in the rat race. But in the long run, unless we are in ongoing communication with God, unless we learn the true meaning of prayer, the rats will win!

### Doing a Reality Check

1. Is it your custom to spend quiet time with God each day? Do you have a special time and a special place for this?

2. Do you find it easier to talk with your friends than with God?

3. Are you completely honest with God? Do you tell Him everything, or just some things?

### Fine-tuning Your Prayer Life

1. Make a list of your daily priorities. Write down how much time you occupy in each activity.

2. What would you have to take out of your life in order to spend special time with God each day? (Remember, when a glass is full, you can't put anything into it. You have to pour out some of the contents first.)

3. Determine that you will spend time alone with Jesus every day (including holidays!).

### *Prayer*

Lord, we spend as much time as we can with our friends and in doing things we like to do. We have tended to spend only enough time with You to squeak by. Please forgive us. We can see now that much that is happening to us is the result of our lack of spending time with You in prayer.

We have made a commitment now to spend quality time with You. Please help us, because it is difficult to form new habits. Remind us when we forget. In Jesus' name, amen.

# Chapter 17

# Keeping Focused

Someone can read the Bible and still be a mean person. Someone can pray and still be a mean person. But a person with the Word of God in their hand and a prayer in their heart cannot be a mean person.

Prayer in essence is communion with God. It is the nourishing umbilical cord that connects us with God. Because prayer is communication with God, it is well to remember the need to keep in focus. Lack of focus is a hazard that is common to all communication. We've all been in conversation with someone who's said to us, "How was that again? I'm sorry; for a moment I lost you." This means that momentarily they may have lost their focus and begun to think of something else. There are several techniques that can help us to keep our focus while spending time with God.

One of the greatest hazards to prayer is sleep! We need to acknowledge this right up front, because when we determine we are going to give God quality time, the devil tries to thwart our good intentions by making us sleepy.

Some years ago in eastern Asia a group of people were called in to have special prayer for someone afflicted by an evil spirit. The devil, it seems, had been speaking through the voice of the possessed person.

I would not recommend what happened next, but apparently the group was taking advantage of the opportunity by asking the devil a question or two. Someone asked him if he ever went to church. Satan replied that he went every week. They then asked him what he does in church, and he admitted he makes people go to sleep. There is no doubt that the devil is a liar and must not be trusted, but that answer surely seems to be true!

After giving a prayer seminar in a certain church, I returned some months later. As I was greeting the people after church, a young man took my hand and told me he had attended the previous seminar. He said that then and there he had determined to spend time alone each day with the Lord. He said the very next day he had gotten up an hour earlier than usual. I asked him how it went, and he responded it was the best day of his life.

I then asked him how it had been going since that time. He confessed with some chagrin that he had been unable to get up early the second day. He said that things had been getting worse, and that now it was difficult for him even to get up to go to work!

It was easy for me to see what had happened to him. That day he determined to spend an hour with the Lord, it was as though the devil had taken a huge tube of Super Glue and squeezed down a long line of it right where the young man slept!

There is no doubt that one of the devil's best tools against prayer is sleep. You are not alone if you find yourself fighting sleep. It doesn't mean you don't love Jesus or that you are insincere or a hypocrite.

Scripture records two important times the devil used sleep to change history. Luke 9:28-33 tells of Jesus taking three of His disciples—Peter, James, and John—with Him up into a mountain to pray. Verse 32 tells it like it was: "But Peter and they that were with him were heavy with sleep: and when they were awake, they saw his glory, and the two men that stood with him." Notice, Jesus takes them up to the mountain to pray and to witness a spectacular glimpse of His glory, and what happens? They go to sleep.

The other sleep that changed history occurred in the Garden of Gethsemene. "He cometh unto the disciples, and findeth them asleep, and saith unto Peter, What, could ye not watch with me one hour? Watch and pray, that ye enter not into temptation: the spirit indeed is willing, but the flesh is weak" (Matt. 26:40, 41).

As a result of their sleeping, the disciples were not able to resist the temptation to flee, and within hours Peter was denying he even knew Jesus.

A person who is serious about prayer will have to deal with sleepiness. Here are some suggestions on how to keep focused and stay awake during the time you spend with the Lord in prayer.

First, consider some physical positions we might assume when we are in our quiet time alone praying to the Lord. This is a valid consideration, because needless to say, getting out of bed and going directly to your knees beside the couch could be just too relaxing.

The way I enjoy praying best is kneeling in the traditional sense. Others who have spent special time alone with God will sometimes prostrate themselves before Him—in other words, down on the face. When I am alone with God, I will often do that.

We may also pray sitting down in a chair or sofa. Sometimes we may find it helpful to pray standing up. We should bear in mind that the physical position we assume in prayer is something we do to express ourselves to Him at a particular moment. The nature and urgency of the prayer often indicates the position we assume.

A word could be said about how we talk with the Lord. We are accustomed to praying out loud when we are in church or with several people, but often many are not comfortable praying out loud when they are alone.

People have told me they don't want to talk out loud in their private prayers because they don't want the devil to hear what they have to say. Personally, I don't care whether the devil hears my prayers or not. He that is in us is stronger than he that is in the world (1 John 4:4)! The devil and I already hate each other, and it can only get worse. I will not let him intimidate me in how I choose to pray. I find that praying aloud when I am alone with God is a very personal experience and actually reminds me of how real prayer is. I don't do this every time I pray, but I do it when I want to. It makes real the words that "prayer is the opening of the heart to God as to a friend." When we are with our friends, we don't just sit around and think together— we talk out loud together! I think it is special to talk out loud to God.

Shall we pray with our eyes open or closed when we are alone with God? Prayer is conversation with God, and in any conversation the mind can tend to wander. When I am praying with my eyes closed and my mind begins to wander, I can bring myself back into focus by opening them. We close our eyes to keep ourselves from being distracted, but if we are distracted by errant thoughts with our eyes closed, there is nothing wrong with opening them to get back on track.

When is the best time to pray? Any time is good, but the best time to begin our prayer life is in the morning. For years it was not my custom to pray in the morning except at breakfast time. It wasn't that I had anything against it, it was just that I had learned from childhood to say my prayers before I went to bed at night.

Experience has taught me otherwise. The prayer at the end of the day is what we offer when the damage has already been done. We have made our mistakes, and it is the time to be sure everything is in order again. But the prayer at the beginning of the day is the "winner's prayer." It is the prayer that puts us firmly on the Lord's side. Then when temptations come during the day, we don't have to wait for a minute to decide whether we are going to yield or not.

How long should we spend with the Lord in the morning? If you have not been spending any time at all, then even a few minutes would be great! Personally, I am motivated by the words of Jesus asking His disciples if they wouldn't pray with Him just one hour. He might have meant at least an hour.

This brings up the practical question of how in the world a person can pray for a whole hour. Spending time alone with God is not intended to be a one-sided conversation. It is a time for contemplation, meditation in its truest definition, inspiration, and education. It is a time in which we devote all our attention to looking at life from God's perspective and allowing the Holy Spirit to transform us into the likeness of the Divine.

One thing we do during the hour alone with God is pray to Him. That means we verbalize our thoughts either in spoken word or in our minds. Another activity could be to write a prayer. There is justification for this. If David hadn't written his prayers, we wouldn't have the Psalms. We all have had experience writing letters to people. If you haven't yet written a prayer to God, I invite you to do so. Some have said that doing this keeps them focused.

Sometimes when I write a prayer to God, I will find a meaningful psalm and copy it. I have on occasion written verses from Scripture in my own words. There are times when I write to Him more formally, using all the biggest and most elegant words I know. Other times I write as His boy and will even sign the prayer, "Your son, Dick." (I am sure each of us wants to be His son or daughter in whom He is well pleased!)

Something else we can do during our quiet time is read the Word of God. I prefer to think of this activity as reading rather than studying the Bible. I read it for sheer enjoyment and inspiration. If I pass you the morning newspaper and invite you to study it, you may say that you don't have time. But if I pass it to you and invite you to read it, you will probably say "Thank you."

Another thing I have found relative to reading the Bible in the morning is that I do not try to read the Bible through. Surely there are many people who make that a project and are blessed by it. On the other hand, others start off on a journey through the Bible, and when they get to Deuteronomy they get bogged down, and the trip may very well stop there. I read the Bible during my quiet time for the sheer joy of it. I look for something that warms my heart. Many have found that the Psalms can be especially meaningful in the morning, although the Gospels are equally inspirational.

Another element many employ during quiet time with the Lord is writing a journal. Some may call it a prayer journal. There are many ways to write a journal. I have found it most useful to record in it my spiritual journey. In my journal I reflect on occurrences with spiritual implication that transpired the day before, or write about an issue that lies heavily on my heart.

The journal becomes a place to reflect and express in writing my questions, as well as the possible answers, that occur to me as I contemplate a particular matter. This way I have solved spiritual issues of enormous importance to me in my journal. You might say that I meditate through my journal.

Many people also keep a prayer list. I have kept through the years what I call a short list that I make up each day. My list doesn't get longer and longer, but tends to reflect my burdens for the particular day. Of course, I have certain things that I pray about every day. For example, I pray every day for my children and grandchildren. I keep two notebooks, one to write prayers in and the other as a journal of my spiritual journey.

Also during my quiet time I read some of the great classics that have to do with prayer or practical aspects of the Christian life. These books inspire and educate me. I do not try to read anything and everything out there about prayer. I prefer to read books on praying to *be* rather than praying to *get*. Of course, it is a matter of personal preference, but I want to know the deep spiritual implications of prayer. I have particularly appreciated the writings of E. M. Bounds and Andrew Murray.

There are so many different things a person can do during the hour alone with God that there may not be enough time to do them all every day. This is not bad, however. Too much of a routine can lose its meaning after a while, and one of the goals of the quiet time is to enjoy it. Our time with the Lord should be fresh every day.

The subject of prayer is very deep and very wide. The Lord will bring prayer to our attention in so many ways in these important days of earth's history if we will but keep in tune. Please don't forget that prayer is the spiritual umbilical cord that connects our hearts to God. Through prayer the wonderful healing grace of the gospel is brought into our innermost being.

This book has said little about answers to specific prayer. Yes, God is answering prayer in a marked way around the world. We rejoice when we hear accounts of the way the Lord is answering prayers. Yet we have discovered that unless we have learned and are experiencing the primary purpose of prayer, which is to seek first the kingdom of heaven and His righteousness, what seems to be an answer from God may in some instances be only a coincidence at best, or worse, a snare from the powers of darkness.

Antivirus programs are installed in a computer to detect and destroy computer viruses, which are programs that have been designed to damage the computer's memory or in other ways to interfere with the efficiency of the one who is operating the equipment. The virus protection program is often running in the background while the computer is on. It analyzes any program that is introduced from outside the computer. If it is determined to be a virus, a warning sounds and the virus is eliminated. I have often thought that this is what the Holy Spirit is to do for us.

When we establish a real prayer connection with God, though we may not always be enunciating words, the Holy Spirit will be like an antivirus program running in the background of our lives. When temptation comes, the Holy Spirit will alert our conscience to the imminent danger, and we will quickly lift our voice to the Lord for deliverance. Then we will know firsthand the meaning of the words "Deliver us from evil."

It is my prayer that your life has been changed as you have read this book. Someone once asked me if prayer does as much good for the person who is praying as it does for those for whom we pray. I replied, "I hope so."

As we pray that the Lord will change the hearts of our loved ones, it is conceivable to us that it might be years before that prayer is answered. Yet as we continue praying for their salvation, our lives become continual personal surrender and victory. Once we understand what prayer is, we can never pray for the salvation of someone without being saved ourselves in the process! We will discover that as we pray the Lord to give our dear ones victory over sin, we ourselves will experience the victory we are requesting for them.

It has been correctly written that prayer is the opening of the heart to God. Prayer is first and foremost about the heart—the hearts of those who pray. In the past we may have used prayer to try to change the world. It is time we used prayer to change ourselves. Someone asked me if it was not selfish to pray for oneself. I replied, "It depends on what you are praying for. If you are praying to win a beauty contest or the lottery, that would be a selfish prayer. But if you are praying that the Lord, though His Spirit, will cleanse you of all selfishness, pride, bitterness and resentment, love of the world, and lust, and in its place give you the fruit of the Spirit, that is not selfish praying at all."

What we see as God's purpose for our lives will determine the focus of our prayers. The Bible tells us God's purpose for our lives. His purpose for your life happens to be the same as His purpose for mine—that we become like Jesus (Rom. 8:29). When the focus of our prayers is that we ourselves would be like Jesus, then we will experience firsthand the meaning of the promise that if we will seek first the kingdom of heaven and His righteousness, all the rest will be added unto us, as well as the promise that all things work together for good to them that love God.

If Peter had prayed, He wouldn't have denied his Lord. Prayer would have prevented David's fiasco. Prayer did protect Joseph. Prayer saved the three Hebrew youth on the plains of Dura. Prayer kept Daniel faithful, and prayer will give us the same victory!

### Contemplation and Commitment

1. Now that you have finished reading this book, how will the concepts you have learned specifically affect the things you pray about?

2. Can you identify components of your lifestyle that are incompatible with your resolve to become a person of prayer?

3. The Word of God is our food, and prayer is our breath. What will you do now to make sure your spiritual life is being nurtured as it must be? Don't forget, our interests are revealed by what we spend time on. For many, their spiritual life is flat or in decline for the simple reason that they are not allocating any time to it.

### Benediction

And now may the Lord bless you and keep you. May the Lord make His face to shine upon you and be gracious unto you. May the Lord lift up His countenance upon us all—our families, our loved ones, even our enemies—and give us peace. Amen.